MW01242282

Life, Love and the Pursuit of Happiness

EMBRACE
— YOUR POWER & —
GO!

Denise Taylor

Host of Life, Love, and Happiness Podcast

www.DeniseTaylor.live

Author's Dedication

**I lovingly dedicate this book to my Mom,
Barbara J. Vinzant.
I'm looking at the highlights. Thank You.**

****

**Everything I do is for us:
Chuck, Chanise & Ciera.**

**My every day is dedicated to our
family. I love you all.**

Special thanks to Vikki Ellison & Cheryl Miller for their help with this project.

Table of Contents:

Introduction

Over 30 years ago, I arrived on a college campus, unsure and uncertain - about everything. I didn't know much about being successful. In fact, many of my experiences up to age 18 were focused on burying childhood pain, trying to fit in, and looking forward to the next good time. School wasn't a priority. Education seemed unimportant. Achievement wasn't even a goal. I was just coasting - undriven and powerless. This reality is a stark contrast to everything I am today. People who know me now can't believe I was ever unmotivated and passive about life. In much the same way, many who knew me back then can't believe who I have become. And guess what?!?!? I am right there with them. I marvel at how much I have changed since I learned to embrace my power.

A series of disappointments that I experienced at a very young age produced a sense of unworthiness in me. Life circumstances delivered relentless blows to my self-esteem that caused me to question my value and led to many bad choices and mistakes. I wasn't much of a scholar. To be honest, I didn't try to be. I wasn't interested in education at all. I was smart, but because education was not emphasized in a way that made it valuable to me, I didn't put forth much effort. The truth is, I was a very witty young woman, strongly logical and could connect the dots quickly. I could hold my own in any conversation and could confidently present and defend my perspective. Because I didn't value education, I skipped school, or I would cut the day short and leave at lunchtime.

Somehow, I managed to make it through middle school and high school, doing just enough to get by. During my senior year of high school, it became very questionable whether I would actually graduate because I had missed so many days of school, lessons, and tests. To me, it wasn't a big deal if I didn't graduate. You see, neither of my older brothers graduated high school and it didn't seem to matter to anyone. So, I thought it wouldn't matter much if I didn't graduate either. Because no one was in lockstep with me or paid attention to my progress in school, I was the only one who knew how unlikely it was that I would walk the stage to graduate. Lacking immediate examples of academic achievement, I was left to fend for myself. My perspective was limited and immature. I didn't know what was possible for me because I had never seen success up close. Yet, there I was, a brand-new freshman on an actual college campus. My life would change forever.

College was the place where I discovered my power. As much as I haven't wanted to admit it … I would have never gotten there without my Mom.

During the spring semester of my senior year, Mom asked me, "So, what are you going to do after high school?" The truth is, I had no idea. I assumed the motive for her asking was because she wanted me out of her house. To get her off my back, I grabbed an answer quickly, "I guess, I'll join the service." Joining the military seemed reasonable enough, since my oldest brother had done that – so I assumed she'd be OK with that response. Honestly, I never had the intention of enlisting; it was simply an answer to make her go away. Mom knew me well enough to know I had no heart for the military - and no plan.

Mom asked me questions to gauge my interests, but I had an attitude! Annoyed and uninvested, I resisted her attempts to steer me in a productive direction. Thankfully, she persevered. She put forth all the effort in helping to guide my future, and I put forth no effort what-so-ever. When Mom asked me about college, I brushed it off because I knew the truth about where things stood in high school. I thought to myself, "Well, it's highly unlikely I'll even graduate from high school and here you are asking me about college." All of this seemed like such a waste of time. But it was her time... so, I was like, "Whatever..."

She forged ahead with her plan "to save me" and I'll be doggone if it didn't work!

Mom would call me into the room to sign college and financial applications. She'd say, "Sign here." Clueless and disinterested, I'd sign, thinking to myself all the while, "They're never going to let me in."

Weeks later, a letter arrived from Miami University. The letter said, "Hello Denise. We are pleased to share that you have been accepted to Miami University on a probationary basis pursuant to participating in the President's Enrichment Program (PEP)."

There I sat ... in SHOCK!

Wait.... What happened? Accepted? Me? I will never forget the day that letter arrived. I was stunned. I sat in a chair staring at it for hours in complete disbelief. But it happened. I was accepted. They let me in.

The Miami University PEP Program was spearheaded by the University's Black Cultural Center with the goal of opening the University's doors to urban students who needed two things: Opportunity and Support.

This opportunity changed my life. The support I received created in me an appetite for success.

I was so green when I arrived on campus. There was so much I didn't know. I didn't understand what a "college" was. I didn't know what a "prerequisite" was. I didn't know what a "major", a "dean", a "residence hall", or a "bookstore" was. Heck, I didn't even know where the campus location in Oxford, OH was until I was taken there and left to give this college thing a try. The list of what I didn't know was long. But there was one thing I did know ... I was finally accepted. And acceptance is what I had longed for all my life.

My world got bigger the instant I arrived at Miami University. I was intrigued and wanted to know more about this new world. For the first time, I felt motivated and curious to discover more about this "accepted" version of me.

I pondered... "Just what could I accomplish if I tried?"

Thankfully, the PEP Program participants were invited to arrive to campus early to help us navigate everything we didn't know. We were exposed to campus life with guidance, given assistance with enrollment paperwork, and we took remedial Math and English classes to strengthen our skills. This was exactly the onboarding process I needed to set me up for academic success.

I'll never forget the program facilitators helping us to get enrolled. They asked me, "What do you want to major in?" And me, cluelessly responding in true ghetto-fabulous form… I responded, "Which one of these majors makes the most money?" To which they said, "The graduates of the School of Applied Science have the highest starting salaries." Then I replied, "Sign me up for that one." The truth is I had no idea what I was saying, doing or even committing to. I knew nothing about Applied Science. I came from a "get money" urban environment so it was the only question I knew to ask. I soon learned that the School of Applied Science was essentially Computer Science. As a major, Computer Science is still one of the toughest studies at any college in the world. It is not the area you'd likely recommend, suggest, or even allow a "barely graduated high school student" to enroll in out of the gate. But they did. And I did.

Thank goodness God has grace for babies and fools. While I started off green, I finished strong. I graduated from Miami University four years later with a Bachelor of Science Degree in Systems Analysis from the School of Applied Science. I landed multiple job offers and graduated with many honors including the Miami University President's Distinguished Student Award, awarded to me personally by University President Paul Pearson in 1992.

Going to college was a defining moment for my life. Everything changed for me. Though going to college didn't erase my past, my experiences, or my mistakes, it gave me a new lease on life to change my days ahead. I started to see what was possible for me. My world became way bigger than anything I had known. And I became more empowered. I was given an opportunity and I seized it. I discovered my power and I embraced it. And I am grateful for the appetite for success that was birthed in me.

It's been well over 30 years since I first stepped foot on Miami's Campus, and I am still grateful for that chance I was given. Though I credit my experiences at MU for helping to stir up a hunger in me for success, and I acknowledge the part I played in making the most of every opportunity, I am fully aware from whom all my blessings flow. God is my Source, and He has allowed me to experience success in every area of my life.

Since attending and graduating from MU, I have discovered certain principles for making success a lifestyle. These are the same principles that I will share with you in this powerful devotional journal. After much consideration of my experiences and achievements, I crystallized the behaviors and mindsets that are critical for success into what I call *Success SuperPower*s. I decided to call them SuperPowers because apart from God, we can do nothing - so when He puts his SUPER on our "natural", our work and who we are becomes "Super Powerful".

The *Success SuperPowers* are principles that are fully Reusable, Transferable, and Reliable. They can be applied to any area of your life for winning results. I have proven them in my own life so many times and they have become my lifestyle. I began to notice a pattern of success when I used these powerful principles to achieve success in life, work, and school. In order for these principles to work, I had to work to see myself successful – being, doing, having and achieving what I desired. I had to shake off fear, though it was inevitable that I would feel afraid and even alone as I charted and pursued new goals. I had to take care of myself because the push to achieve success demanded a lot; I could not afford for my health to be compromised in the process. And finally, I had to hold fast to my faith. God had so many promises for me that ensured I could indeed do, be, have and achieve.

These perspectives were needed regardless of the success I desired – life, love, career, finances, and more. Whatever the goal, I know I must: (1) See Myself Successful, (2) Shake Off Fear, (3) Do The Work, (4) Take Care of Me, and (5) Hold Fast To My Faith. I also discovered that the Success SuperPowers are activated by three key Power Boosters - Commitment, Consistency and Confidence.

People often ask, "Denise, how do you do it?"

Simply put, I embrace my power. While it requires activation of the power boosters I mentioned - Commitment, Consistency and Confidence, the Success SuperPowers will change your life. They are the necessary steps to Embrace Your Power.

I have reached the point where I want to transcend being *successful* to being *significant*. For me, significance occurs when you willingly invest your time, talent, and resources for the benefit of others. My goal is to help you change your life for the better. I want to help you seize your moment … much like I did many years ago.

- Denise

My Prayer for You…

Heavenly Father – I thank you for the significance of this moment and I pray that you bless the one holding this book right now. I am asking for the loving, protecting, and enlightening power of your Holy Spirit to engulf them with everything they need to persevere. I pray for clarity to be revealed as they pursue Your call. I pray for witty ideas to be birthed through them. I pray for peace to be a constant as they seek to be who you are calling them to be. Even more God, I pray that you give them a keen vision to see themselves successful, courage to shake off fear, tenacity to do the work that is needed, perspective to make taking care of themselves a priority, and grit to hold fast to their faith. I know that you can do it for them God – because you have been faithful to do it for me. Father, I pray they know, accept, and believe that you have not given them a spirit of fear but of power, love, and a sound mind. May they Embrace their Power and Go, now! In Jesus' name I pray. Amen.

Life, Love and the Pursuit of Happiness

EMBRACE
— YOUR POWER & —
GO!

Unpacking the Success SuperPowers:

The Success SuperPowers are principles that are fully <u>Reusable</u>, <u>Transferable</u>, and <u>Reliable</u>. They can be applied to any area of your life for winning results. They are activated by three key power boosters - Commitment, Consistency and Confidence.

- **Commitment**: the state or quality of being dedicated to a cause, activity, etc.
- **Consistency**: the achievement of a level of performance that does not vary or diminish greatly in quality over time.
- **Confidence**: a feeling of self-assurance arising from one's appreciation of one's own abilities or qualities.

<u>Success SuperPower #1</u>
"See Yourself Successful"

Your vision sets the goal. You must SEE the accomplished version of yourself. If you're struggling to SEE yourself being, doing, having, or achieving what you desire, then you're likely unconvinced you can have it. Vision is the critical first step as it sets the stage for what is possible for you. Saturating your mind with seeing the "Possible You" sets your belief. Once you can see it, you can believe it, and you are ten steps closer to achieving it. Visualizing can begin simply by allowing yourself to daydream about it. I say "allowing" because we are often so steeped in the reality of our circumstances that we have forgotten how to let go and just dream. Dreaming is a way to mentally stretch to SEE more than what you're experiencing with your senses. It's an effective strategy that helps us grasp what can be and who we can become.

You should spend time daily with the "Possible You." Get to know her very well - how does "Possible You" look, act, respond, show up, work, believe, interact, invest and more. It is empowering to SEE you doing what you want to do. There are many resources you can use to further train your mindset, but nothing beats seeing yourself in action. I love how Apostle I.V. Hilliard puts it - "We must visit our future on the canvas of our imagination." Seeing ourselves being, doing, having, and achieving is a MUST to shift our mind to believe in what is possible for us.

Things like pictures, vision boards, affirmations, declarations, visiting spaces and places that represent your dream, as well as talking with someone who is achieving what you desire – are excellent methods that can help you see yourself in your successful future.

We must see ourselves strong.
We must see ourselves victorious.
We must see ourselves successful.

Success SuperPower #2
"Shake Off Fear"

Almost every successful person begins with two beliefs – (1) the future can be better than the present and (2) they have the power to make it so. Likewise, every person that has achieved anything has one more thing in common – they have all faced fear and persevered. Fear is a natural response to change. When we are challenged in any way, fear sets in … even if it's just for a second. It's the reality of uncertainty that makes us gasp and wonder a number of things - like "can we do it", "are we ready", "is it possible", and "am I good enough." These questions and many more begin to surface when we are faced with the possibility of our vision. In fact, if the thought of your vision doesn't evoke any semblance of fear, your vision is too small.

Fear is nothing more than **F**alse **E**vidence **A**ppearing **R**eal. We must remove all doubt and choose to turn our *can'ts* into *cans* and our dreams into plans. We must nurture our ability to shake off fear until it becomes an innate part of who we are without having to try or to think about it. I realize that shaking off fear is far easier said than done. When I battle fear, I focus on this truth, "God did not give us a spirit of fear. He gave us power." And with that power, we can be, do, have, and achieve.

Here's something I absolutely love about success… It's Personal. You get to choose what you want your success to be – you decide how big, how wide, and how high. Your success has NOTHING to do with anyone else. Nothing is too big, too wide, or too high for God to make happen for you. You don't have to be afraid to go for success as you please. If it aligns with God's Will, it can be yours. It's simply a matter of your faith – not your fear.

Doubt is a form of fear, and God did not give that to us. God gave us power and we must embrace it fully. Doubt lurks in our mind, warring against the belief that success is possible for us. To win against fear, we must strengthen our belief and think on these things.

> "Finally, brothers and sisters, whatever is <u>true</u>, whatever is <u>honorable</u>, whatever is <u>right</u>, whatever is <u>pure</u>, whatever is <u>lovely</u>, whatever is <u>admirable</u>—if anything is <u>excellent</u> or <u>worthy of praise</u>—think about such things." Philippians 4:8

Fear doesn't stand a chance when we're convinced that success is possible. Fear doesn't stand a chance when we believe we can.

Shaking Off Fear is about restricting doubt from running rampant. It will show up, but we can't forget: We have command of our mind, and we can "pull rank." You are empowered to determine what goes on in your mind! When doubt creeps in, that's when we must make an intentional response to think on what is true, honorable, right, pure, lovely, admirable, excellent, and worthy of praise. When you chasten your mind to think these things…doubt will flee, and fear is shaken off.

"Do The Work"

I believe in declarations, affirmations, and confessions. Yes… we should "Name it" and "Claim it." Yes… we should "Speak It" and "See it." Yes… we should "Blab it" and "Grab it." Give me every strategy and I will use it to drive my faith forward. We must speak affirming words and build our faith. These practices are powerful and necessary. The principles of speaking faith words are indeed incredible and life changing, but success takes more than words alone. While confessions are a part of my personal lifestyle, I know faith without works is dead. Experience has taught me, repeatedly, that success is something you must WORK for – not just hope for. It is only in doing the work that our faith comes alive.

Our faith is made known more by what we do than what we say. Faith is an action word. I know we hope for the easy route, but the reality is that you must work to bring your vision to pass. The good news is our labor comes with a promise. God promises to bless the work of our hands.

So, the question is, "What are you DOING?" What have you given God to bless?

It's sad … really heartbreaking, to see so many great ideas unpursued; so many great books unwritten; so many great speeches unspoken; so many great songs unsung; so many great inventions just left on paper; so many great relationships unmended; so many degrees unobtained, and so many great dreams unrealized. Yes, we receive the vision, and we may even go as far as speaking and writing the vision – yet the work of the vision often remains undone.

When I was a kid, I would sometimes watch this show called, "Bewitched." The main character on the show was a good witch and with the twitch of her nose, she could make things happen. Whatever was needed would appear or it would occur. Unfortunately, it has never been that easy for me, though I have often wished it was. Going to college took work. Getting promoted took work. Getting my MBA took work. Starting my businesses took work. Launching my podcast took work. Writing my books took work. Being married for 27+ years took work. And raising our two girls took work. While these are only a few of the things I've been blessed to accomplish, I want you to know all the rest of the things took work, too.

Success requires your effort. You must put your hands to the plow and get it done. Do something daily that moves you forward to the "Possible You." Never be afraid of going slow - but be very afraid of standing still. You are possible. But you must do the work.

11

"Take Care Of You"

There is a mantle of greatness tied to everything God inspires. I'll admit it's heavy and demanding. When we are called to achieve, we take on a lot. And when we take on the demand of the call in our own strength, we will be overwhelmed. Chasing the dream can wear you out. What is needed from you will never let up. Therefore, it is critically important to "Take Care Of You." When you are driven, finding the "off" button is hard. We can go, go, go – sometimes to our detriment. Driving ourselves hard feels like the right thing and our intentions are good, but we must implement a strategy of self-care.

Listen… self-care is far more than manicures and pedicures. It's really sad that we have reduced our personal care to the exterior alone. Those things are fine, but they lack the substance needed to truly sustain the weight of greatness you possess and the success that awaits you.

Developing a self-care strategy requires that you invest in yourself fully so that you can perform optimally. It's a conscious act to promote your own physical, mental, and emotional health. It means seeking the necessary help, support and partnerships that edifies you and build you up - mind, body, and soul.

I have personally learned the value of prioritizing my needs. I have accepted that I am worth the investment. I hit a wall during the pandemic that made me double down on what was necessary for me to thrive. I have a huge capacity which simply means I can juggle a lot. It is normal for me to have to wear many hats and maintain many balls in the air all at once. In fact, this characteristic is not unique to me as it is common with high achievers. When the demand kicks in, we hit "the zone." The reality is the zone feels good to us – almost like a natural high. The other reality is this level of drive is heavy, but we are often not aware of the weight - until it's too late.

During the pandemic, my Mom took ill, and I had to step in and become her full-time caregiver in addition to my normal load of responsibilities. That's when I felt my knees buckle for the first time. I realized that simply adding all of her needs to my own jam-packed list was not going to work. While I had occasional self-care items peppered into my schedule, I soon discovered the value of creating a holistic strategy for taking care of me. I also discovered I had been missing out on really prioritizing my needs by not regularly addressing all of me – mind, body and soul. I became intentional about my walks to free my mind, massages to relax my body, therapy to process my growing demands, vacations to stimulate my peace, healthier eating to fuel my body, and meditation to anchor myself in God. I hired staff to help carry the administrative load. And yes, I still get my toes and nails done, too. All of these things are mainstays because I now understand how much better it makes me show up – in fact, it saves me.

Self-care is often overlooked, yet it is vital for building resilience to bear the life stressors you cannot eliminate. When intentional steps are taken to care for yourself fully, you'll be better equipped to live your best life and diligently pursue "Possible You.".

"Hold Fast to Your Faith"

"Hold Fast To Your Faith" is not the last Success SuperPower because it's least important – in fact, it is the most important. The Bible has so many promises for us but they all must be received by faith. Faith is confidence in what we hope for and assurance about what we do not see. (Hebrews 11:1) We must remain confident and assured – that is faith.

Faith is easy when things align. We don't rely on faith much when things are going well. It's during the days of contradiction when our faith is tested, that we discover its true value and power of steadfast faith. We understand the necessity of faith on the days when we know the promise, know what we believe, and we've worked hard … yet things still aren't coming together as we planned. Faith is what we lock in when we are disconnected, and it seems our goals are distant. It is our confidence and assurance of what we cannot see.

Apostle I.V. Hillard is by far one of the best faith teachers I've ever experienced. Whenever I need my faith energized, I go straight to his teachings and devour them to build my faith. He teaches when we are in faith, we have five justifiable expectations of God:

    (1) We can expect God to give us a plan of action,
    (2) We can expect the wisdom of God,
    (3) We can expect the favor of God,
    (4) We can expect a miracle from God (the supernatural to occur), and
    (5) We can expect strength to endure until change comes.

I have discovered the power of holding fast to my faith which is standing in full expectation for God to show up in one or more of these ways to help me. This is what it means "to be *in* faith." Hold onto your faith.

We cannot get weary in pursuing God's will for us. Anything worth having is absolutely worth your pursuit, worth your diligence and worth your passion. Do not give up when you face opposition as it's often a sign that success is near. Stay focused on your goals, believing it is possible for you.

The world needs your deposit. There are people waiting for you to show up strong. So, don't let delays confuse your objective or dilute your commitment. Stay the course. Your decision to pursue "Possible You" may be challenged but it is not a mistake. Success is imminent. Don't give up. Don't ever give up.

Life, Love and the Pursuit of Happiness

EMBRACE
— YOUR POWER & —
GO!

How to get the most from this experience:

This 30-day journey is designed for women who desire more success in any area of their life. This comprehensive guide has a focus for each day. Every day you will Read, Reflect, Affirm, Journal, and Set Goals.

- The daily readings are intended to motivate, inspire, challenge and prompt reflection. As a backdrop, always keep your personal goals in mind. Think about "Possible You" and what you want to achieve. This book is designed to support you in every season. You may find that it speaks and inspires you differently in different seasons. So, keep it handy and in rotation throughout the year.

- The affirmations are most impactful when they are read out loud. We shift our mindset more quickly when we speak it and hear it rather than just reading them in silence. Modify them to best suit you. Make them personal.

- Focusing on the Success SuperPowers you need most each day will help you embrace your power. Spend time understanding the Success SuperPowers so you can know where to step up your game. Combine them with the power boosters: **Commitment, Consistency and Confidence** for impactful change in you.

- Reflecting on your success goals daily helps to keep them in front of you. If you're like me, you may discover new aspects of your goals or even discover new goals as you reflect. This section is intended to keep your goals at the forefront of your thoughts and keep you energized and focused on pursuing them. Whatever is revealed to you, capture it by writing it down so it's handy in your hot pursuit to achieve.

- Intentionally identifying how you will embrace your power - based on the day's success principle - will drive your empowerment. Don't hold back. Capture even the little things by writing them down in your journal. It is significant for both excellence and consistency to include everything that comes to mind.

Your first challenge is to prioritize your time for this experience. Share with your family and close friends that you are committing to a growth process, and you need their support. Share with them that this is a 30-day journey, and you are committed to focus. Identify a daily 30–60-minute window of time when you are at your best, to work through this process. Protect your committed time. Get up early or stay up late. Avoid choosing a window of time when you're fatigued. You deserve to experience what you can deliver when you are at your best.

Before you start: I want to affirm that YOU are worth the investment of your time and commitment to this process. Sometimes we get weary in well-doing and fail to finish strong. We cannot struggle with consistency but expect strong results. Make a commitment to yourself to see this process through to the end. Nothing beats the experience of accomplishment. And on top of all that, you will benefit personally, professionally, and relationally. You will BE the change you want to see. You will Embrace Your Power.

"POSSIBLE YOU"

See Yourself Successful

Discovering more about what you SEE when you See Yourself Successful is where "Possible You" begins. It is an essential place for us to start.

I have a key role as your coach & champion, but I cannot define "Possible You" for you.
I will indeed encourage you to go for it!
But exactly what IT is – is up to YOU.
Just know you're good enough
to have whatever you see, and
God is big enough to make it happen.

Possible You is Possible for You.

I believe you can be, do, have, and achieve ANYTHING your heart desires.

So, before we jump in, let's discover more about "Possible You"

"Write the vision, and make it plain upon tables, that he may run that reads it.
Habakkuk 2:2

The Bible admonishes us to write the vision & make it plain and that is the absolute best place to start. This will set the stage for this entire journey in the most powerful way.

WHAT DO YOU SEE?

What would happen if ALL limitations were removed?

What would you be?

What would you do?

What would you have?

What would you achieve?

This is where you get to remove every excuse, eliminate every consideration of feasibility & likelihood and free your mind to visualize who you would be if all limitations were gone.

How do you look?

How do you manage things?

What would be more? / What would be less?

Where would you be? / What does that place look like?

How would you describe "Possible You"?

Capture your VISION of "Possible You"

Be detailed and include pictures that may help you visualize. Don't hold back. Dream. Get to know more about her. As you discover more about her on this journey, come back and update the vision.

Success SuperPower #1
See Yourself Successful

_____

_____

_____

_____

_____

_____

_____

_____

_____

_____

_____

_____

_____

_____

_____

_____

_____

_____

_____

_____

_____

_____

_____

_____

_____

_____

_____

_____

_____

_____

_____

_____

_____

_____

_____

_____

_____

_____

_____

_____

_____

_____

_____

_____

_____

_____

_____

_____

_____

_____

Life, Love and the Pursuit of Happiness

EMBRACE
— YOUR POWER & —
GO!

Start Where You Are

(Day 1)

Do not despise these small beginnings, for the LORD rejoices to see the work begin.
- Zechariah 4:10

Your Season is Now! Whatever your goal, start where you are, using what you have, and doing what you can.

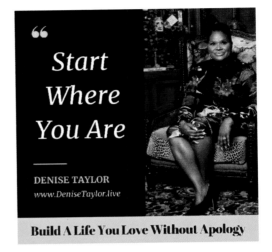

Don't let doubt keep you stuck. Success absolutely takes diligence and effort. But more than that, it takes a *start*. It requires you moving forward on the vision in your heart. As long as there are no efforts made, your goal will never be achieved. You are worth the effort. You deserve it.

You can do it!

Let's get started, today and slay some goals! It's time to overcome & achieve.

Embrace Your Power & Go!

Today's Affirmation: (edit the words as needed & speak it confidently out loud):

Starting TODAY, I take wise, strategic, and powerful steps toward my goals, with the Spirit of the Lord, vision, and purpose as my guide. I embrace small beginnings as seeds of unlimited potential and rejoice with the Lord to see the work begin, knowing that He will bless the works of my hands and cause all that I do in faith to prosper.

Which Success SuperPower do you need to tap into most today? (check all that apply)

- **See Yourself Successful**
- **Shake Off Fear**
- **Do The Work**
- **Take Care of You**
- **Hold Fast To Your Faith**

What did you discover about your Success Goals?

_____

_____

_____

_____

_____

How will you Embrace Your Power & Go today?

_____

_____

_____

_____

_____

Just Checking In…

Getting started is often the hardest part. For me, this is where I need to leverage SuperPower #1 most often – "See Yourself Successful."

Once I can visualize myself doing it, being it, having it or achieving it – then things seem to settle, and the vision becomes possible for me. I wish I could say this is something that you'll only need to do once, but the truth is you will need to intentionally "see yourself successful" very often. Once your imagination is captivated by what is possible for you, then you'll be relentless about your success. Soon those three power boosters (Commitment, Consistency, and Confidence) will kick into overdrive - and you will soar.

I'm reminded of when God nudged me to start the <u>Life, Love and Pursuit of Happiness</u> podcast. It was something I never imagined I'd be doing – let alone love doing it. Before there was ever an episode, I visualized sitting with my guests, stepping to the mic, and sharing in wonderful conversations. I visualized greeting them and even closing out the show with my signature Life, Love, & Happiness questions. I saw it long before it ever came to pass, and it captivated me. That vision motivated me to get out of the starting blocks and launch the show. Seeing yourself successful makes it possible for you to see your dream as a reality. It helps you to believe.

If Not You, Who? If Not Now, When?
(Day 2)

And who knows whether you have not come into the kingdom for such a time as this?
- Esther 4:14

When I was younger, I entered a speech contest. After winning local and state competitions, I made my way to the National Competition in St. Louis, MO with a black history speech that my mom helped me to prepare. The mark of a great speech is a powerful ending. My compelling proclamation at the end was, *"If not you, who? If not now, when?"* My goal with this speech was to compel the listeners to take personal action.

That very phrase came to mind when I thought of you, today. I thought of how you sometimes question yourself and put off the success you desire. I thought of how you somehow believe you have time on your side though it keeps on ticking into the future. I thought of how you so often consider the interests of others ahead of your own.

Believe me, I only know your thoughts because they have often been my own. These are the very same thoughts I've used to hold myself back, to shrink, to stay comfortable. They were also the same thoughts I had to cast aside so the greatness in me could fully emerge.

I get it. I understand what you're going through. I've been there. I had to discover the courage to believe in me and put myself first.

Hey Sis! Greatness is in you, too. Yes, it's your time to soar.
So today, I admonish you the same way I did those listeners long ago...
If not you, who? If not now, when?
Embrace Your Power & Go!

Today's Affirmation: (edit the words as needed & speak it confidently out loud):

I am the answer to someone's silent prayers. I have the solution to someone's most conflicting dilemma. I am the distinctly designed, virtuously vested, and specially chosen by God for this very day, for this unique era and moment in time. I am the blueprint. My legacy begins today. *If not me, who? If not now, when?*

Which Success SuperPower do you need to tap into most today? (check all that apply)

- **See Yourself Successful**
- **Shake Off Fear**
- **Do The Work**
- **Take Care of You**
- **Hold Fast To Your Faith**

What did you discover about your Success Goals?

_____

_____

_____

_____

_____

How will you _Embrace Your Power & Go_ today?

_____

_____

_____

_____

_____

Just Checking In...

It's easy to procrastinate and hope the divine nudge to act will go away. I'm not sure why, but we foolishly convince ourselves that putting things off will make the call to do, be, have, or achieve go away. In full transparency, I tend to put things off when I'm a little scared of how I will need to stretch and grow personally to get the job done. Going for it usually requires me to GROW for it. That's why SuperPower #2 is critical to success – we must "Shake Off Fear." What's at the heart of why you are putting things off? Understanding this will help you become more intentional and loosen the grip of fear.

Ain't No Stopping You Now...

(Day 3)

For God has not given us a spirit of fear,
but of power and of love and of a sound mind. - 2 Timothy 1:7

There is nothing more powerful than YOU with a made-up mind!

You can *Achieve*.
You can *Become*.
You can *Possess*.
You can *Do*.
You are *Success*.
You are *Unstoppable*.

God has not given You a spirit of FEAR. He gave you Love, Power and a Sound Mind. You are FREE to SOAR!

Embrace Your Power & Go!

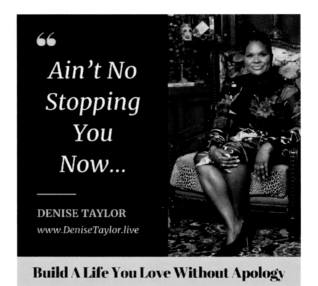

Today's Affirmation: (edit the words as needed & speak it confidently out loud):

> I am unstoppable because God has given me power, love, and a sound mind. I am empowered to overcome every obstacle. I am loved beyond limits. I can achieve the impossible because I have the mind of Christ.

Which Success SuperPower do you need to tap into most today? (check all that apply)

- **See Yourself Successful**
- **Shake Off Fear**
- **Do The Work**
- **Take Care of You**
- **Hold Fast To Your Faith**

What did you discover about your Success Goals?

_____

_____

_____

_____

_____

How will you _Embrace Your Power & Go_ today?

_____

_____

_____

_____

_____

Just Checking In…

I love quotes. They serve as instant reminders to me. My working spaces are peppered with them, my journals have them on the covers, and I store them on my phone. Having them as "Pick Me Uppers" keeps me focused and confident. I keep them accessible and go straight to them when I need to be energized. Quotes are more than fancy words; they are strategies to help me stay steady and in hot pursuit. What we feed ourselves is critically important. It is the fuel we use to build and maintain our mindset. Success SuperPower #1 – "See Yourself Successful" needs the daily addition of positive, powerful, prolific proclamations to keep the vision clear. Today, I want to share one that has always captivated me.

"Our deepest fear is not that we are inadequate. Our deepest fear is that we are powerful beyond measure. It is our light, not our darkness, that most frightens us. Your playing small does not serve the world. There is nothing enlightened about shrinking so that other people won't feel insecure around you. We are all meant to shine as children do. It's not just in some of us; it is in everyone. And as we let our own lights shine, we unconsciously give other people permission to do the same. As we are liberated from our own fear, our presence automatically liberates others." – Marianne Williams

If You Know Better... Do Better.

(Day 4)

Making the most of the time [buying up each opportunity], because the days are evil.
- Ephesians 5:16

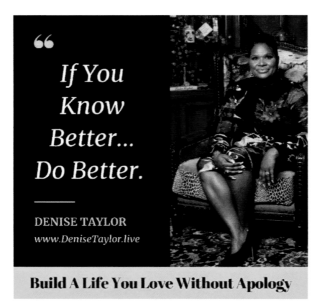

It's incredible to consider many of us have likely lived more than half of our lives. As I process that truth, I admonish you to put purpose into the time you have left.

I know my BEST days are ahead. I have more legacy to build for my children and my children's children. I cannot waste any more time. It's just too precious and valuable.

It's TIME for Extraordinary Living. It's time to Build a Life You Love Without Apology.

Living extraordinarily often makes those around you uncomfortable. Your shine will likely expose the limitations that bind others around you. So, as you thrive, expect hints of discontentment from those closest to you. With focused resolve, we must accept the fact that everyone cannot go with us, nor will they fully understand our desire for more. To this, I say:

Go ANYWAY.
Pursue ANYWAY.
Become ANYWAY.

No more wasted time! Live your life on purpose. *Embrace Your Power & Go!*

Today's Affirmation: (edit the words as needed & speak it confidently out loud):

> **I live a life of extraordinary focus and passionate purpose. My children and my children's children will eat the fruit of my legacy and glean from a life well-lived. I have full expectation that my latter days will be greater than my former days because of the glory of God that is upon my life.**

Which Success SuperPower do you need to tap into most today? (check all that apply)

- **See Yourself Successful**
- **Shake Off Fear**
- **Do The Work**
- **Take Care of You**
- **Hold Fast To Your Faith**

What did you discover about your Success Goals?

_____

_____

_____

_____

_____

How will you *Embrace Your Power & Go* today?

_____

_____

_____

_____

_____

Just Checking In…

I recently had a conversation with a young lady that used to babysit my children. She shared how she was just letting life pass her by. It is as if she was waiting on someone or something, yet she couldn't name it. My heart broke because I knew she was letting her best days slip right through her fingers. Regardless of our age, WE DESERVE TO LIVE FULLY. Building a life we love is not about things – it's about fulfillment. It's about refusing to settle when you can do, be, have or achieve what you want. When you embrace your power, you can build a life you love.

Faith Won't Work Unless You Do
(Day 5)

In the same way, faith by itself if it is not accompanied by action, is dead. - James 2:17

Faith is indeed an action word. In fact, proof of our faith is seen by what we do. While believing is super critical to achieving, we must go further and align our actions with our belief in order to achieve.

Have you ever "heard" someone say one thing, yet you "see" their actions contradict their words? They say they want to lose weight, yet their eating habits don't align with their stated desires. They say they want to save money, yet their spending habits don't align with their words. They say they want to excel professionally yet their work habits don't align with their goals. They say one thing and do another. In those cases, their words are not proven by their actions and their faith is not seen.

Listen, we absolutely should "Name it" and we absolutely should "Claim it". But it's only in the "Doing" that our faith comes alive. Faith is made known more by what we do. It's true... Faith won't work unless you do. So, do something that aligns with what you're believing in God for today. Show up strong.

Embrace Your Power & Go!

Today's Affirmation: (edit the words as needed & speak it confidently out loud):

> **My daily actions demonstrate my faith. Today, I take strategic, decisive, and intentional action towards my purpose and my goals. My thoughts, words, decisions, and actions are in full alignment with what I believe.**

Which Success SuperPower do you need to tap into most today? (check all that apply)

- **See Yourself Successful**
- **Shake Off Fear**
- **Do The Work**
- **Take Care of You**
- **Hold Fast To Your Faith**

What did you discover about your Success Goals?

_____

_____

_____

_____

_____

How will you *Embrace Your Power & Go* today?

_____

_____

_____

_____

_____

Just Checking In...

Dear Heavenly Father,

Thank you for your grace, mercy, and peace. We owe our lives to you. You chose us. We are grateful for your patience with us. We are thankful for your forgiveness. God, please help us strengthen our hope in you. We get weary and sometimes face unfortunate circumstances, but you are the help we need. You are our provision. Help us to trust fully. As we pursue the greatness you have called us to accomplish, help us be willing partners. Give us favor for open doors and opportunities. Thank you for loving us. Thank you for redeeming us. In Jesus' Name. Amen.

Success SuperPower #5 – ``Hold Fast To Your Faith'' isn't last because it's the least important. It's last because it is most important. There will be dark days as you forge ahead – it is faith that will help you through. There will be days of contradiction – it is faith that will help you through. There will be days filled with struggles – it is faith that will help you through. I've faced many of those days - rejection, denial, death, job loss, foreclosure, bankruptcy, and more. It was faith that helped me through. Faith is most important...so hold fast to it.

You Can Handle It!
(Day 6)

I can do all things through Christ who strengthens me. - Philippians 4:13

Square your shoulders, Baby!

You are built to handle the pressure that comes with your calling. Yes, it looks larger than life, it feels heavier than weights, and it's more demanding than you feel capable of taking on. But it's still YOUR calling all day and your prosperity is tied to breaking through any obstacle you may face.

You are empowered to do it. You are graced for your purpose. So, set yourself FREE to soar.

A BIG Calling requires BIG Courage, which relies on your unshakeable faith. The best acronym for FAITH is *Forsaking All, I Trust Him.* That sums it up! Even though what you're facing may seem bigger, heavier, and more demanding, your faith assures that you will receive the supernatural strength to get the job done.

Efforts over Excuses. Always.

Faith over Fear. Always.

Embrace Your Power & Go!

Today's Affirmation: (edit the words as needed & speak it confidently out loud):

Because FAITH is my choice, FREEDOM is my portion. Forsaking All, I Trust Him. I trust God with my life, my dreams, even my disappointments. I am strengthened by God's promise and through Christ, I have assurance of victory.

Which Success SuperPower do you need to tap into most today? (check all that apply)

- **See Yourself Successful**
- **Shake Off Fear**
- **Do The Work**
- **Take Care of You**
- **Hold Fast To Your Faith**

What did you discover about your Success Goals?

_____

_____

_____

_____

_____

How will you _Embrace Your Power & Go_ today?

_____

_____

_____

_____

_____

"Thomas Edison's teachers said he was "too stupid to learn anything." He was fired from his first two jobs for being "non-productive." As an inventor, Edison made 1,000 unsuccessful attempts at inventing the light bulb. When asked, "How did it feel to fail 1,000 times?" Edison replied, "I didn't fail 1,000 times. The light bulb was an invention with 1,000 steps."

"POSSIBLE YOU"
Shake Off Fear

Discovering more about what's holding us back takes courage. Many times, the "things" causing us to shrink and limit ourselves are rooted in fear. Shaking off fear sounds way easier than it is. Many of us have found comfort and security in our limiting beliefs and playing small. God created us for greatness, yet we don't always have experiences that build us up to achieve. So, we comfortably cower and tell ourselves it's OK. To achieve we must decide to be courageous. We may have to face past hurts, mistakes, disappointments and possibly even forgive ourselves for poor choices and situations we've mishandled. To begin and sustain the journey to becoming 'Possible You" we must Shake Off Fear.

You are good enough to have what you see and God is big enough to make it happen.

Possible You is Possible for You.

Be strong and courageous. Do not be frightened, and do not be dismayed,
for the Lord your God is with you wherever you go.
Joshua 1:9

WHAT ARE YOU FEARFUL OF?

What happened to dilute your perception of your potential?

Who do you need to forgive?

Do you need to forgive yourself?

What is the truth?

What is a lie?

What boundaries or standards need to be set?

What support or help will make a difference now?

Getting a life coach was one of my best decisions. Having someone dedicated as my listening ear and guide, reminding me what God says about me, has been instrumental in me truly embracing my power. I am a strong advocate for getting help – be it a therapist, coach, or counselor. Their ability to help us process our fears and past traumas is an effective fear shaking strategy. God provides help for all areas of our life.

What is *really* holding you back?

What is stopping you from becoming "Possible You"?

It's likely past hurts, words, experiences, and maybe even traumas may be holding you back. Those experiences tend to make us devalue how we see ourselves and dilute what we believe is possible for us. As you discover more on this journey, come back, and update your fears. Knowing them will help you be more targeted with your prayers and empower you whenever you sense fear rising.

Shake Off Fear

_____

_____

_____

_____

_____

_____

_____

_____

_____

_____

_____

_____

_____

_____

_____

_____

_____

_____

_____

_____

_____

_____

_____

_____

_____

_____

_____

_____

_____

_____

_____

_____

_____

_____

_____

_____

_____

_____

_____

_____

_____

_____

_____

_____

_____

_____

_____

_____

Life, Love and the Pursuit of Happiness

EMBRACE
— YOUR POWER & —
GO!

Evolve Or Repeat... You Choose

(Day 7)

Therefore, if anyone is in Christ, he is a new creation. The old has passed away; behold, the new has come. - *2 Corinthians 2:15*

Every day you are presented with two choices: Evolve or Repeat.

Remaining the same discounts your purpose, downplays your greatness and disregards your strengths. It ensures you'll keep getting the same meager results over and over again. Only CHANGE will create a new thing and invite new results. It is only when you change that you release your greatness and soar to new heights. Only change begets change.

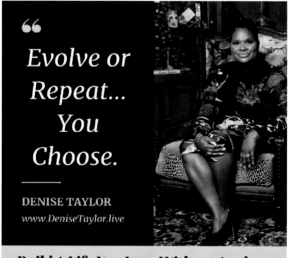

In order to achieve more, become more, or do more - we must stretch, grow and advance beyond our limiting beliefs. Evolve and embrace change like your future depends on it, because the fact is - it does!

Embrace Your Power & Go!

Today's Affirmation: (edit the words as needed & speak it confidently out loud):

Today, I choose to evolve and embrace change in my life in order to become the person God designed me to be. I release former attitudes, limiting mindsets, and mistakes of the past to walk in my greatness and soar to new heights in the purpose for which God has prepared me.

Which Success SuperPower do you need to tap into most today? (check all that apply)

- **See Yourself Successful**
- **Shake Off Fear**
- **Do The Work**
- **Take Care of You**
- **Hold Fast To Your Faith**

What did you discover about your Success Goals?

_____

_____

_____

_____

_____

How will you _Embrace Your Power & Go_ today?

_____

_____

_____

_____

_____

Just Checking In…

I decided to Evolve.

For the longest time I felt there was something more I should be doing. It wasn't as if my life wasn't full – my to-do list was long, yet I still desired meaning and purpose as many do. As I embraced my power once again, I found my voice. I settled my mission and began to soar. This new sense of fulfillment was addictive and I wanted to serve.

My mission is simple… I am here to encourage, motivate, inspire, implore, demand, convince, boost, reassure, beseech, plead, urge, strengthen, spur and compel YOU to Build A Life You Love Without Apology. Discovering your power to do so will likely mean dealing with stuff (and possibly people) that have held you bound. I know this can be painful, overwhelming, and even embarrassing to revisit. But don't be dismayed. God didn't give us a spirit of fear. He gave us Power. We can Embrace Our Power & Go. As sure as my name is Denise, I believe we deserve Success and Happiness in Life & Love.

When you think of YOUR EVOLUTION … What Do You See? I saw inspiration through service, empowerment, and happiness. Identifying your vision will lead to fulfillment. I've learned that clarity comes in the doing. So, it's best to just start where you are - doing what you see.

Spring Forward Indeed!
(Day 8)

I press toward the mark for the prize of the high calling of God in Christ Jesus.
- Philippians 3:14

Have you ever thought about what it will look like when you truly make the decision to "Do You"? How will your life transform when you begin to say "yes" to yourself? It's time for you to shine. It's time for you to Spring Forward.

There were times in my life when I settled for less and sold myself short. I would even shrink to stay in a place of comfort. Though I secretly wanted more, I always found a way to talk myself out of pursuing it. To be transparent, I remained stuck because I refused to see myself successful, gave into fear, didn't want to do the work, didn't believe in myself, or gave up too soon.

Can you relate? The moment I decided to be honest with myself and give up my excuses, my greatness emerged. I began to Spring Forward! Today, I also challenge you to put your excuses to the side and walk in your greatness. You don't have to wait until a certain time of the year. This is your moment. It's time for you to blossom. It is, indeed, time for you to Spring Forward.

Embrace Your Power & Go!

Today's Affirmation: (edit the words as needed & speak it confidently out loud):

> **Today, I make the quality decision to let go of my excuses and move beyond every limiting comfort zone. I see myself successful. I choose faith over fear. I do the work. It's my time to Spring Forward and I will Spring Forward, indeed!**

Which Success SuperPower do you need to tap into most today? (check all that apply)

- **See Yourself Successful**
- **Shake Off Fear**
- **Do The Work**
- **Take Care of You**
- **Hold Fast To Your Faith**

What did you discover about your Success Goals?

_____

_____

_____

_____

_____

How will you *Embrace Your Power & Go* today?

_____

_____

_____

_____

_____

Just Checking In…

One of the things that held me back for many years was the unfortunate circumstances I experienced as a child. My innocence was taken, and I was left holding the bag, trying to figure out what to do with the damage caused to me at the hand of those who should've protected me. I was deeply impacted. My self-esteem was tarnished. My sense of worthiness was clouded. My willingness to love fully was severely diminished.

Unfortunately, I buried it. I buried the chaos and the pain. I buried it deeply within me and just tried to move on. And it seemed to work - until it just didn't anymore. I was forced to come face to face with what happened to me. It was as if I couldn't move forward until I began dealing with the pain that I tried to keep locked away.

To others… I looked fine, performed well, and achieved measures of success. But I knew the truth all the while … my real truth. I was bound. I was shrinking, holding back, and hiding in plain sight. When I finally had the courage to spend time reckoning with "what happened to me," I discovered that it did not ruin the essence of who I am. It is hard as hell to face all those hellish experiences. It has taken lots of help, prayer, and fortitude. If your experiences are the same, I want you to know: What happened to you did not ruin you. You're Good, Sis.

We All Need A Mr. Miyagi

(Day 9)

As iron sharpens iron, so one person sharpens another. - Proverbs 27:17

I love the movie "Karate Kid". I love the original, the sequels and the remake Will Smith did with his son. I appreciate how the movie shows the power of relationship - how shared experience and partnership can empower one to aspire, achieve, and provide wisdom to address matters that overwhelm.

I really love Mr. Miyagi, the sage martial arts and life coach. His role was critical to helping Daniel, the main character and young martial arts mentee, discover his own power. Mr. Miyagi guided Daniel through both traditional and unconventional steps to explore his strengths, enthusiastically cheered him on, and built his confidence. Mr. Miyagi's mentorship indeed accelerated Daniel's achievement. Mr. Miyagi's leadership and Daniel's willingness to learn are the Success SuperPowers I strive to both to share and exemplify.

The truth is we were not meant to try to achieve success alone. Though the magic of cinema dramatics made it seem like Daniel stumbled onto Mr. Miyagi by chance, I believe our connection is more transformational and divine. We are connected for a reason - a very empowering reason. I am here to encourage you, but more than that, this is a partnership. Not all partnerships are equal. Partnership that is built on the foundation of experience and wisdom promotes mastery and accelerates success.

Thanks for being connected with me. *Embrace Your Power & Go!*

Today's Affirmation: (edit the words as needed & speak it confidently out loud):

I open myself up to powerful partnerships. I actively seek out and cultivate relationships that are fruitful, positive, authentic, and mutually beneficial. As iron sharpens iron, I am blessed with mentors, friends, associates, & mentees that sharpen me, as I sharpen them. I have the wisdom and confidence to release relationships that make me dull and do not bear good fruit. Goodness, mercy, and great relationships pursue me all the days of my life.

Which Success SuperPower do you need to tap into most today? (check all that apply)

- **See Yourself Successful**
- **Shake Off Fear**
- **Do The Work**
- **Take Care of You**
- **Hold Fast To Your Faith**

What did you discover about your Success Goals?

_____
_____
_____
_____
_____

How will you *Embrace Your Power & Go* today?

_____
_____
_____
_____
_____

Just Checking In…

 *When you can find someone to partner with you on your journey - that is a blessing. I am thankful for so many who played key roles in my life. I have a number of friends, co-workers, and leaders who have invested in me personally. I've even had mentors who coached me from afar. Bishop T. D. Jakes mentored me from a distance. I would wake up early and spend focused time devouring every teaching of his I could get my hands on. It was Bishop Jakes who helped me 'get loosed' from pain and he pushed me to embrace my power. Who has mentored you? Reflect on their best lesson.*

Faith Over Fear

(Day 10)

For whatever is born of God is victorious over the world; and this is the victory that conquers the world, even our faith. - 1 John 5:4

This is a moment of truth for us in many areas of life, right now - a test of what we truly believe. Keeping your focus steady in a rapidly changing environment is hard.

Our daily lives have been shifted. Business and the economy seem uncertain. The threat of sickness continues to lurk in the atmosphere. To all that I say, we must continue to hold on to our faith. If we are going to make it through these times, faith is a must.

Faith is your confidence. It's your steady belief that good will prevail. It's your hope and motivation to see beyond today's cloudy reality.

Yes, decisions need to be made to navigate whatever you're facing. Know that you are graced to make the moves that matter. Steady yourself and make the decision to choose faith over fear.

There are many acronyms used to break down the meaning of fear, but my fav is **F**alse **E**vidence **A**ppearing **R**eal. I refuse to believe false appearances. I know the truth about me and Who I serve. I believe that God is working all things together for my good. This is still true even when it doesn't feel good or look good. It will always go well for me. Even in trying seasons, it's ok, 'because I'm built to last. So are you! A winner is in you. Giving up is not an option.

I admonish you, now more than ever, to hold tight to your faith. Let your faith rise and overshadow every fear.

Embrace Your Power & Go!

Today's Affirmation: (edit the words as needed & speak it confidently out loud):

I live from a place of victory. Today, I choose faith over fear. My faith is anchored in God, not in what I see or how I feel. All things are working together for me. I am born of God, victorious, overcoming, triumphant over fear. Yes, I choose FAITH!

Which Success SuperPower do you need to tap into most today? (check all that apply)

- **See Yourself Successful**
- **Shake Off Fear**
- **Do The Work**
- **Take Care of You**
- **Hold Fast To Your Faith**

What did you discover about your Success Goals?

_____
_____
_____
_____
_____

How will you *Embrace Your Power & Go* today?

_____
_____
_____
_____
_____

Just Checking In…

 *Doubt has a way of creeping in when we're closest to achieving. I know this well because I battle it when I am right on the brink of a win. It can be very consuming, but that is when we must level up our thinking. How do we level up our thinking? Well, there is a Word for that: Philippians 4:8! When doubt creeps in, we must make an intentional response to think on what is true, honorable, right, pure, lovely, admirable, excellent and worthy of praise … and doubt will flee.*

Use Time Wisely

(Day 11)

Teach us to number our days, that we may gain a heart of wisdom. - Psalm 90:12

Yes, things are different. And if we're honest we can now identify many things that have cluttered our spaces and our calendars. You have likely noticed that many of those things you thought you "just had to do" are not as necessary as you may have once believed. Some things were a necessity, but many really were not.

Now that life has slowed and has been stripped down to the basics, our most valuable commodity has been revealed... TIME. Many of us who complained about not having enough time, are oddly the same ones who now complain about the abundance of time we have on our hands. Don't the mistake of failing to recognize the gift of this moment.

Here are some truths about TIME:

- You need it.

- It never looks back; it always keeps moving forward.

- You can't control it; you just get to use it.

- You get the same amount as everyone else, so it is distributed fairly.

- It's more valuable than money because you can't grow it or earn it - you only can spend it.

- And once you spend it, you can't get it back.

How you spend your time is so critically important to your overall wellbeing. Successful people have learned the value of time and they don't waste it. Instead, they are intentional and protective of the moments of their lives. Take full advantage of the current season we are in. Don't waste your time with worry - instead, use this time to pray, rest, reflect, and plan your next move. Ask for wisdom for the current time and the days ahead.

Embrace Your Power & Go!

<u>**Today's Affirmation: (edit the words as needed & speak it confidently out loud)**</u>

I commit to making the most of my time. I choose to seek wisdom instead of sinking into worry. As I pray, rest and plan, I am confident that greater days are ahead for me.

Which Success SuperPower do you need to tap into most today? (check all that apply)

- **See Yourself Successful**
- **Shake Off Fear**
- **Do The Work**
- **Take Care of You**
- **Hold Fast To Your Faith**

What did you discover about your Success Goals?

_____

_____

_____

_____

_____

_____

_____

_____

How will you *Embrace Your Power & Go* today?

_____

_____

_____

_____

_____

_____

Right Now Plan
(Day 12)

Now faith is the substance of things hoped for, the evidence of things not seen.
- Hebrews 11:1

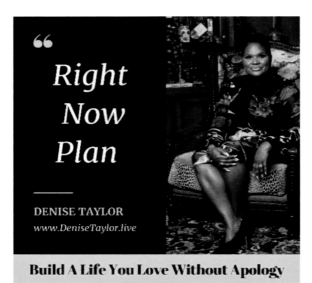

I had an amazing conversation with a young lady I interviewed yesterday. She said something that made me love her vibe instantly. She said, "Everyone keeps asking me about my 10-year and my 5-year plan. All that's fine, but I'm focused on my RIGHT NOW plan."

I so wanted to interrupt her and say "Woot! There it is," as she asserted her power so confidently. In that moment, I could sense her resolve, determination, and commitment. She had faced a lot of changes over the last year, including a job-related transition due to the pandemic. In spite of all this, she found the power to own her moment.

All I could do was smile as I savored the good look of confidence on her face. She showed up to our interview a bit grungy and casual from her work at a local ballpark. It reminded me of the classic scene in the movie Pursuit of Happyness where the main character, Chris Gardner, played by Will Smith, showed up for his life-changing interview after being released from jail, with paint splattered all over his clothes. Nevertheless he, like my young interviewee, seized the moment.

You see, we all face circumstances and conditions that have the potential to profoundly impact and even degrade our sense of worth and self-esteem. But in every situation, we are presented with a choice. We can all choose our attitude and how we will show up. Will we go "low" or go "high" concerning our lives? Will we seize our moments and own them fully? Will we leverage the great opportunity that every moment holds?

Make showing up powerfully and courageously a part of your RIGHT NOW plan.

Embrace Your Power & Go!

Today's Affirmation: (edit the words as needed & speak it confidently out loud)

My RIGHT NOW plan is to make the most of every opportunity that is in alignment with my purpose. I will show up with boldness, courage, and power. My circumstances do not define me. I am beautifully clothed in grace, strength, and limitless potential.

Which Success SuperPower do you need to tap into most today? (check all that apply)

- **See Yourself Successful**
- **Shake Off Fear**
- **Do The Work**
- **Take Care of You**
- **Hold Fast To Your Faith**

What did you discover about your Success Goals?

_____

_____

_____

_____

_____

How will you *Embrace Your Power & Go* today?

_____

_____

_____

_____

_____

Just Checking In…

Seizing the moment and saying yes is one of the HARDEST things to do. On the other end of that "YES" is uncertainty. Yet it is only through seizing moments that you can experience change. I once heard a Pastor share, "God gives you more on the way than he does at the start." I have found that to be true in my life, many times. Whether starting a new job, relocating to a new city, launching a new business, or getting married and having kids, God has been faithful to "be there" in every moment. It's the reality of that uncertainty that makes SuperPower #5 valuable – "Hold Fast To Your Faith." When I'm vulnerable, I take refuge in God's love and grace. It's secure and constant.

"POSSIBLE YOU"
Do The Work

Vision is demanding and requires work. There is a huge misconception that things can happen without sweat and effort. But the truth is we must get in the game and put our hand to the plow. I've discovered "God gives us more on the way than He does at the start" which means He'll bless what we begin. Getting out of the starting blocks is critical to God showing up on our vision's behalf. To me, it makes sense that He wants to see us doing our part as we have a key role to play in bringing the vision to pass.

We must begin doing the work.

While the 3 key power boosters are relevant for all the Success SuperPowers, they are critically necessary when it comes to doing the work.

- **Commitment**: the state or quality of being dedicated to a cause, activity, etc.
- **Consistency**: the achievement of a level of performance that does not vary or diminish greatly in quality over time.
- **Confidence**: a feeling of self-assurance arising from one's appreciation of one's own abilities or qualities.

Remember – You are good enough to have whatever you see, and God is big enough to make it happen.

Possible You is Possible for You.

The LORD will send a blessing on your barns and on everything you put your hand to. The LORD your God will bless you in the land he is giving you.

The LORD will open the heavens, the storehouse of his bounty, to send rain on your land in season and to bless all the work of your hands.
Deuteronomy 28:8,12

What does POSSIBLE YOU need most?

What things are priority? What things are less important?

What resources are necessary?

What can you begin NOW?

What clarity is needed?

WHAT WORK IS REQUIRED OF YOU?

What work is needed to become "Possible You"?

If you're like me, I can think of a lot of things to do but getting clarity on what is necessary, and the priority requires quality "thinking time". Also, consider examples – those who are achieving as you desire – not to copy them but to start your thought processes on what work you may need to begin. Consider how you want to show up. Rushed efforts often lessen excellence so pay attention to details as you do the work. As you discover more on this journey, come back, and update this list.

Success SuperPower #3
Do The Work

_____

_____

_____

_____

_____

_____

_____

_____

_____

_____

_____

_____

_____

_____

_____

_____

_____

_____

_____

_____

_____

_____

_____

_____
_____
_____
_____
_____
_____
_____
_____
_____
_____
_____
_____
_____
_____
_____
_____
_____
_____
_____
_____
_____
_____
_____
_____

Life, Love and the Pursuit of Happiness

EMBRACE
— YOUR POWER & —
GO!

The New Normal

(Day 13)

Do not remember the former things, Nor consider the things of old. Behold I will do a new thing… - Isaiah 43:18-19

Here's the truth: Things will never be the same after 2020. So, if you're waiting for things to go back to the way they were before, you're gonna struggle. Everything that has happened was intended to disrupt our "normal." This excites me! Change is good … and necessary. When many of us faced circumstances that required us to shift quickly, our excuses fell hard.

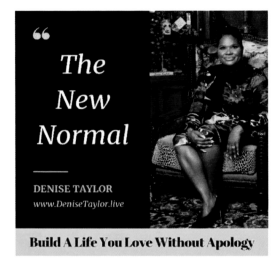

We were forced to think creatively. Companies and households are making decisions faster than ever now. Decisions that once took months are now being made within hours. New business ventures that used to take months, are now launching within days. The micro-management leadership style has given way to trusting employees to execute their tasks from home. Undervalued service roles – teachers, nurses, grocery clerks, delivery workers – are now celebrated and recognized for their true significance. I'm telling you a NEW NORMAL has emerged and it's about time.

If you are still stewing because things are not the same, it's time to get into motion. If you do not get in step with the changes that are occurring in this era, chances are that you, your business or ministry will become a relic of the past. Relevance and consistency are absolutely necessary in order to thrive in these changing times. Do the Work.

Embrace Your Power & Go!

Today's Affirmation: (edit the words as needed & speak it confidently out loud)

Nothing catches me unaware. I am well-equipped for these changing times and can pivot effectively when necessary. My ear is pressed up against the heart of God and I move according to His leading. I can confidently embrace change because my steps are ordered.

Which Success SuperPower do you need to tap into most today? (check all that apply)

- See Yourself Successful
- Shake Off Fear
- Do The Work
- Take Care of You
- Hold Fast To Your Faith

What did you discover about your Success Goals?

_____

_____

_____

_____

_____

How will you *Embrace Your Power & Go* today?

_____

_____

_____

_____

_____

Just checking in…

As we settle into what life will be, it's very important to "Take Care Of You." Success SuperPower #4 is the one that often gets discounted or dismissed. When in reality, YOU are a very key aspect of your success. When I think about what our family faced in the pandemic season, I am grateful for the new experiences that I made mainstays for me – therapy, vacations, massages, delegation, meditation, and relaxation were a few things that I layered into my days to SAVE ME! Be intentional about what YOU need. Life is limited without you at your best. Success is limited without you enjoying it fully. What self-care mainstays do you need to add to your days in order to show up stronger and take care of you?

Purpose Creates Urgency

(Day 14)

For it is God who works in you to will and to act in order to fulfill his good purpose. - Philippians 2:13

My purpose keeps me busy! This last week has been all abuzz with demands and responsibilities. Honestly, it's a lot of pressure. But I love every minute of it because I'm thriving in my purpose. My daily mission is to rise above all excuses and make every effort to pursue my calling. There are many things that happened this year that were outside of my control. However, my purpose did not change. My determination relies on me doing my part to operate faithfully and consistently in my purpose and entrusting all other things to God.

The same is true for YOU. Your purpose has not changed. No person, virus or warning to stay home can change what God has planned for you. In fact, the events and subsequent impacts of the pandemic should have stirred up a greater sense of urgency in you to GO! Your deposit is needed - your gifts, your knowledge, your insight. You are VERY necessary for this season and the season yet to come. The world can't afford you playing small. Pursue your purpose faithfully and with urgency.

Embrace Your Power & Go!

Today's Affirmation: (edit the words as needed & speak it confidently out loud)

> **Daily, I execute my purpose with a sense of urgency and excellence. I am a seed planted in the earth by God. My deposit in the world is necessary, therefore I will rise to the occasion, no matter the obstacles in my way. The Spirit of God is actively at work in me to do all that He has called me to do.**

Which Success SuperPower do you need to tap into most today? (check all that apply)

- **See Yourself Successful**
- **Shake Off Fear**
- **Do The Work**
- **Take Care of You**
- **Hold Fast To Your Faith**

What did you discover about your Success Goals?

_____

_____

_____

_____

_____

How will you *Embrace Your Power & Go* today?

_____

_____

_____

_____

_____

D O U B T

Create In Me A Clean Heart
(Day 15)

Create in me a clean heart, O God; and renew a right spirit within me. - Psalm 51:10

We have so much to be thankful for.

That statement can stand-alone but oftentimes we won't let it.

We allow our experiences to weigh in on the truth of that statement. We view gratefulness through a distorted lens, magnifying all of the things that have gone wrong in the world. As we move our attention from what is good and right, our attitude and demeanor become marred with discontentment and ungratefulness. Before you know it, we start "feeling some type of way'" and you can't even see anything to be thankful for.

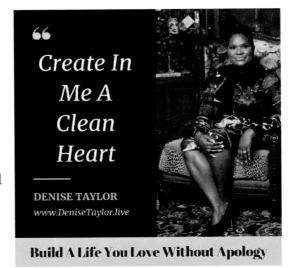

Human beings have an unfortunate tendency to internalize all the wrong stuff and reject what is good. We cling to our painful experiences though joy is available. Left unchecked, our heart fully adopts bitterness as its normal state, without even needing the jaded lens anymore.

My prayer is that the Lord would create a clean heart in us so that we can be refreshed and see His goodness instead of our pain. May we see possibilities instead of the flaws. May we see potential instead of fears.

In order to truly SOAR and build a life we love, we must be willing to do the heart work, which is indeed the hard work. We must confront the distorted lens that prevents our hearts from seeing that life is good.

Embrace Your Power & Go!

Today's Affirmation: (edit the words as needed & speak it confidently out loud)

Lord, my deepest desire is for You to create in me a clean heart of gratefulness that sees the good in life. Renew a right spirit in me that always expects the best. I yield to You, Lord, to do the heart work, which is often the hardest work of all. I surrender my limited perspective to gain Your peace and joy. In Jesus' Name. Amen.

Which Success SuperPower do you need to tap into most today? (check all that apply)

- See Yourself Successful
- Shake Off Fear
- Do The Work
- Take Care of You
- Hold Fast To Your Faith

What did you discover about your Success Goals?

_____

_____

_____

_____

_____

How will you _Embrace Your Power & Go_ today?

_____

_____

_____

_____

_____

Just Checking In...

I know what it feels like to be overwhelmed. I also know what it's like to process through it. And while it requires mental toughness to stand against the attacks - it also requires humility to remain open to God when we can't see our way, or when we don't like how we feel about something or someone. We are called to impact the world. And everything God is looking to accomplish in that quest, He will do through us. Surrendering to Him requires that we be open to His will. We must keep our hearts ready to serve. We must stand and show up strong. Are you ready?

<u>Your Imagination Is Your Only Limitation</u>

(Day 16)

What no eye has seen, nor ear heard, nor the heart of man imagined, what God has prepared for those who love him … - 1 Corinthians 2:9

I'll admit I haven't always allowed my imagination to soar. I have often pulled back, giving way to fear and a limiting sense of inadequacy. My confidence was weakened by my life experiences. My lack of belief in myself made my resolve even weaker. I still battle against stinking thoughts of unworthiness and feelings of inferiority, but now I have strategies to fuel my faith.

I build my faith by imagining the very best for myself and my family. I intentionally replace limiting thoughts with big dreams. I exchange negative words from myself and others with audaciously positive language. I resolve to no longer be denied. I resolve to stop playing small. I resolve to Go For It - and I'm on a mission to help others do the same.

Build A Life You Love Without Apology.

<u>**Today's Affirmation: (edit the words as needed & speak it confidently out loud)**</u>

I am all of that! I refuse to let the past and current circumstances get the best of me. Truth is, I am a bad mama-jamma! I am resourceful, creative, and successful. Every day I am discovering my strength and it's POWERFUL. I celebrate my unique abilities. I am gifted to make a difference, be a blessing, and to shine brightly in this world.

Which Success SuperPower do you need to tap into most today? (check all that apply)

- **See Yourself Successful**
- **Shake Off Fear**
- **Do The Work**
- **Take Care of You**
- **Hold Fast To Your Faith**

What did you discover about your Success Goals?

_____

_____

_____

_____

_____

How will you _Embrace Your Power & Go_ today?

_____

_____

_____

_____

_____

Just Checking In…

I NEVER SAW ME COMING…

It's funny how people can see you now and think your days have been easy simply because you're successful. "But my life ain't been no crystal stair…" I had some hard stuff I had to get past to truly embrace my power.

I had to settle what was important to me and then see the life that I wanted. I had to shake off every version of fear that would rise – doubt, insecurity, low self-esteem, and my tendency to shrink and remain behind the scenes. I had to do the work – the hard work – of catching up to excel. I had to find the right rhythm to take care of myself and release all the baggage I was carrying. I had to stick with it when I didn't want to give up – those times when things were so hard to endure and even face.

It's not that successful people don't quit, get frustrated, or experience failure. We do - often. But what makes us successful is we get back in there until we see it work. We don't take losses – we get lessons. I didn't start out this way. I trained myself to be committed, consistent, and confident. And you can, too. It begins with "Possible You" – she MUST be dope enough to make you want to become all she is. Develop your thirst. God can satisfy it.

Dreams Don't Just Come To Pass, They Must Be Planned & Worked

(Day 17)

For the dream comes through much effort, and the voice of the fool through many words. - Ecclesiastes 3:5

The only thing that beats a dreamer is a dreamer with a plan and a willingness to work. Visions don't just come to pass, they come through effort. We must plan the work and work the plan to achieve our dreams.

One of the most strategic elements of any success plan is seeking the counsel of an advisor or a coach. Creating a plan to achieve your dream can be a daunting endeavor. A great coach can help you sort through the details to make your dream reality.

Success requires a strategy. Though a quarterback has the instinct to lead the team and run the plays, he still recognizes the insight and wisdom of the coach. Every great quarterback relies on the mentorship, play development, and perspective of their coach to help them win the game.

While talking to your friends and family may get you cheers, talking to a coach will get you to your goal. Let me help you get in the end zone. You and your dreams are worth it.

Build A Life You Love Without Apology.

Today's Affirmation: (edit the words as needed & speak it confidently out loud)

My dreams are worth the work. Today, I commit to my own success. I will invest faith, time, work, and resources into the fulfillment of my dream. I plan for what I expect. I trust as if it all depends on God. I work as if it all depends on me.

Which Success SuperPower do you need to tap into most today? (check all that apply)

- **See Yourself Successful**
- **Shake Off Fear**
- **Do The Work**
- **Take Care of You**
- **Hold Fast To Your Faith**

What did you discover about your Success Goals?

_____

_____

_____

_____

_____

How will you *Embrace Your Power & Go* today?

_____

_____

_____

_____

_____

Just Checking In…

Ok, I'll admit it… I was lazy.

Learning to "Do The Work" was hard. I know it's easy to walk away from things that are not fulfilling OR do not have a meaningful purpose attached to them. It just is and I've done it, too. Understanding your "WHY" is important as it becomes the reason for all efforts to follow. "No Meaningful Why" = "No Interest to Work"

Consider this: in high school, I had a dropout mentality and behavior, yet while in college I graduated with the University President's Distinguished Student Award. I can tell you I arrived on campus … the same lazy Denise I had been for the four years prior. Four years later, my name was being called for achievements I never imagined. What changed? I found a "WHY" that was meaningful enough to me and it compelled me to go hard. Yes, there were many other factors that supported my collegiate success, but the single most impactful thing that made a difference is that I changed my mind about ME. I saw myself successful and I liked what I saw. Even still, the "WHY" did not give a free pass from having to do the hard work to earn my degree in computer science. But the "WHY" awakened everything in me that I surrendered to laziness before. Is your "WHY" compelling enough for you to do the hard work?

What Are You Waiting For?

(Day 18)

He who observes the wind will not sow, And he who regards the clouds will not reap.
- Ecclesiastes 11:4

I have two questions for you: (1) *What exactly are you waiting on?* (2) *Why are you waiting on that?*

We are so good at putting off what we want and settling for an excuse. Excuses are easy and don't require much work. Successful people don't make excuses, nor do they allow circumstances to stop them. They rise to the occasion. Excuses are reasons given by people who don't really want to do the work required to be successful.

In order to live the life you want, you must intentionally choose effort over excuses until action becomes your norm. Stop putting off your dreams. Now is the time.

Build A Life You Love Without Apology.

Today's Affirmation: (edit the words as needed & speak it confidently out loud)

Today I choose effort over excuses. Intentional action is my norm. I am among the successful who rise to the occasion, above doubts, circumstances, and obstacles. I faithfully do the work necessary to achieve my dreams. Now is my time.

Which Success SuperPower do you need to tap into most today? (check all that apply)

- **See Yourself Successful**
- **Shake Off Fear**
- **Do The Work**
- **Take Care of You**
- **Hold Fast To Your Faith**

What did you discover about your Success Goals?

_____

_____

_____

_____

_____

How will you *Embrace Your Power & Go* today?

_____

_____

_____

_____

_____

Just Checking In…

We must overcome this crazy notion of needing validation. It's disheartening how we seek it from others. So, here's the post: <u>Validation is for Parking!</u>

You are enough. With God, You are MORE than enough.

I was trapped in that swirl - hoping to hear from someone that "I was good enough" or "Yes, it's OK" or "Yes, you can." The silly thing is God already said all those things long ago – yet we're still asking and ignoring His Word. We only look for validation when we're NOT doing what we know we should. Deep inside we know we are not showing up fully. Our asking is a subtle stall tactic we often use under the guise of gaining acceptance or even seeking permission. It's a way of shrinking, hoping others will confirm that they see what we already saw.

Look… God said what He said. His word is enough and so are you.

For the longest time I secretly wanted more. I often found myself shrinking to fit in, settling for what was comfortable and even selling myself short. Once I finally accepted that we deserve success and we are blessed with power to achieve it, I stopped playing small. I'm serious about building a life that I love, and you should be too."

*Sound familiar?!?! It's from the podcast. I mean it every time: **Embrace Your Power & Go!***

"POSSIBLE YOU"
Take Care of You

We have poor habits that fail to take care of who we are – physically, spiritually, financially, and emotionally.

We are so willing to take the short end of the stick and doing so drains us and often robs us of becoming who we want to be. What do I mean… we often deprioritize our needs for the interest of others, we often go without so others can have, we often settle so others can do and worse of all we forsake ourselves, our dreams, and our voice when we fail to prioritize them. We foolishly believe that those actions "keep peace" yet they terrorize us on the inside while others seemingly get what they want at our expense.

"Possible You" requires that You stand up for You.

You must believe YOU are worth standing up for and YOU must take the stand.

Taking care of yourself is way more than a stash of cash on the side in case he leaves. It's more than a day here & there labeled as a "Me Day" to treat yourself special. It's more than an occasional "Girl's Night Out" for laughter and fun. It's more than a mani & pedi or even your monthly massage at Hand & Stone. It's more than a new pair of shoes or whatever your retail therapy choice may be. And it's more than looking pretty in the mirror at an outer appearance that fails to radiate from peace within. Now don't get me wrong, I consider these things valuable experiences but **taking care of you requires more depth**.

Taking Care Of You is an intentional strategy that covers all areas of you – where you consider all factors according to <u>YOUR</u> best interest and make decisions with <u>YOU as a priority</u>.

It's a plan that builds and edifies you wholistically with intentional effort.

Beloved, I pray that you may prosper in all things and be in health, just as your soul prospers.
3 John 1:2

How does your soul need to prosper?

What have you downplayed, ignored, or deprioritized concerning you?

How do you need to build yourself up? How are you weakened & being held back?

WHAT AREAS NEED MORE FOCUSED ATTENTION?

How does "Possible You" need you to take better care of you?

Sacrifice requires us to go deeper than we thought but was never intended to be to our detriment. How do you need to be restored so that you are valued and can take care of yourself wholistically? In what areas and ways have you been taking the short end of the stick? What specific areas need to be strengthened? What decisions or actions need to be stopped? What help do you need now?

<u>Success SuperPower #4</u>

Take Care of You

_____

_____

_____

_____

_____

_____

_____

_____

_____

_____

_____

_____

_____

_____

_____

_____

_____

_____

_____

_____

_____

_____

_____

_____

_____

_____

_____

_____

_____

_____

_____

_____

_____

_____

_____

_____

_____

_____

_____

_____

_____

_____

_____

_____

_____

_____

Life, Love and the Pursuit of Happiness

EMBRACE
— YOUR POWER & —
GO!

Dream It. Wish It. Do It.
(Day 19)

Now to him who is able to do immeasurably more than all we ask or imagine, according to his power that is at work within us. - Ephesians 3:20

Your tiny realistic goals may entertain you but leave no room for God.

God wants to do abundantly more and exceed even your grandest expectations. So, if you can wrap your mind around how to make it happen, it's likely NOT big enough for God to get involved.

Think of what you desire and then multiply it by 1,000 - maybe then you might create a little room for Him to jump in. I believe that He desires even greater for us than what we've imagined. Push past your limits and stretch your thinking to His level.

It's time to stop playing small. We can no longer shrink to the lie that we are not enough. When we believe the lies, we discredit God! Increase your willingness to dream. Be curious. Explore. We often say nothing is too hard for God, but we fail to act as if that is true.

Building a Life You Love Without Apology requires grit, courage, and belief. If the vision doesn't scare you, it's too small for God. He loves to show off and show out on your behalf. Join Him in the work by dreaming bigger.

Today's Affirmation: (edit the words as needed & speak it confidently out loud)

Today, I will take God at His Word and expand my capacity to dream. I will push past the limits of my imagination and stretch my expectation so wide; it will require the intervention of heaven to bring it to pass. All honor and glory to Him who is willing and able to do exceedingly, abundantly far over and above all I can dare ask, hope, dream, or imagine. In Jesus' Name. Amen.

Which Success SuperPower do you need to tap into most today? (check all that apply)

- **See Yourself Successful**
- **Shake Off Fear**
- **Do The Work**
- **Take Care of You**
- **Hold Fast To Your Faith**

What did you discover about your Success Goals?

_____

_____

_____

_____

_____

How will you _Embrace Your Power & Go_ today?

_____

_____

_____

_____

_____

keep going...
keep going...
keep going...
keep going...
keep going...

Are You Under The Influence?
(Day 20)

Do not be deceived, bad company corrupts good character. – 1 Corinthians 15:33

Build A Life You Love Without Apology

Are you under the influence? Truly, each of us is influenced by someone. We put a lot of value in the opinions of others. That is why we must be very conscientious about who we allow in our circle. Our associations make a lasting impact on who we are and what we do. The Bible says it this way, "Bad company corrupts good character." In the words of my father-in-law: "If you have 9 broke friends, you'll be the 10th".

Pay keen attention to the conversation and actions of the company you keep. Those who are close to us feed our eye gates and our ear gates, and they influence us more than we realize. Doubt can start as a seed in the form of a seemingly innocent comment from someone we love and trust.

Gathering opinions is only necessary for surveys and polls – not our dreams. When it comes to our dream, opinions mean far less than our purpose. We must assess all we hear according to wisdom and truth. Does what you are hearing sharpen you to pursue your purpose or is it a distraction? Is your circle truly vested in your success or are they attached to you for their own gain? Are those in your circle looking to the future or are they stuck in the past? Have they given up on their dream and made it their business to talk you out of yours? Assess your circle! Who's influencing you?

Build A Life You Love Without Apology

Today's Affirmation: (edit the words as needed & speak it confidently out loud)

I select my associations wisely. I conscientiously choose the company of those who dream audacious dreams and do the work to achieve them. My circle is made up of men and women of stellar integrity, tenacity, and faith. They sharpen me daily, hold me accountable, and help me to guard my focus – and I do the same for them.

Which Success SuperPower do you need to tap into most today? (check all that apply)

- See Yourself Successful
- Shake Off Fear
- Do The Work
- Take Care of You
- Hold Fast To Your Faith

What did you discover about your Success Goals?

_____
_____
_____
_____
_____

How will you *Embrace Your Power & Go* today?

_____
_____
_____
_____
_____

Just Checking In…

My father-in-law passed away while my husband and I were still dating. He was full of little sayings that I still remember, though my time with him was short. It's funny how his warning about "9 broke friends" has stuck with me after all these years. It made me seriously consider the company that I kept. But even more, it made me consider the potential impact of being the company of "9 rich friends" instead. I'm grateful for the stellar company of friends, colleagues, and associates that God has afforded me to connect with. I recently did a "Tips From the Top" podcast series to tap into the experiences of those who have achieved professional success. Check it out.

Your Playing Small Does Not Serve

(Day 21)

Let your light so shine before men, that they may see your good works, and glorify your Father which is in heaven. - Matthew 5:16

What an incredible mark of unity and success the 2020 Inauguration was for me. I felt included, represented & connected. I felt empowered, considered and challenged. Most of all, I felt proud.

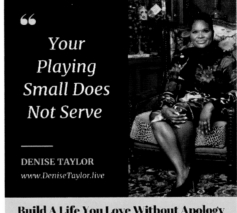

Build A Life You Love Without Apology

I was reminded of an inspirational passage by Marianne Williamson that I read often to encourage myself. I would like to share it with you, today.

"Our deepest fear is not that we are inadequate. Our deepest fear is that we are powerful beyond measure. It is our light, not our darkness, that most frightens us. Your playing small does not serve the world. There is nothing enlightened about shrinking so that other people won't feel insecure around you. We are all meant to shine as children do. It's not just in some of us; it is in everyone. And as we let our own lights shine, we unconsciously give other people permission to do the same. As we are liberated from our own fear, our presence automatically liberates others."

Thank you, Marianne Williams, for these words that challenge us to rise and be. Seeing the light of our nation radiate compassion and understanding is liberating.

Embrace Your Power & Go!

Today's Affirmation: (edit the words as needed & speak it confidently out loud)

I will shine my light to its full brightness, today. I will seize every opportunity to live big in this world. The earth needs what I have to offer. I will employ every gift, talent, ability, and skill to help others and bring glory to my Father in Heaven.

Which Success SuperPower do you need to tap into most today? (check all that apply)

- **See Yourself Successful**
- **Shake Off Fear**
- **Do The Work**
- **Take Care of You**
- **Hold Fast To Your Faith**

What did you discover about your Success Goals?

_____

_____

_____

_____

_____

How will you _Embrace Your Power & Go_ today?

_____

_____

_____

_____

_____

THE HARDEST THING TO DO IS LEAVING YOUR COMFORT ZONE. BUT YOU HAVE TO LET GO OF THE LIFE YOU'RE FAMILIAR WITH AND TAKE THE RISK TO LIVE THE LIFE YOU DREAM ABOUT.

Just Stick With It

(Day 22)

And let us not be weary in well doing: for in due season we shall reap, if we faint not.
- Galatians 6:9

Do not get weary!!! Anything worth having is absolutely worth your pursuit, your diligence, and your passion. Do not give up when you face opposition, as this is often a sign that success is near. Stay focused on your goals. They are meaningful and necessary.

The world needs your deposit. There are people waiting for you to show up strong. So, don't let delay confuse your objective or dilute your commitment. Stay the course. Your decision to pursue may be challenged, but it is not a mistake. Success is imminent and it sure looks good on you.

Embrace Your Power & Go!

Today's Affirmation: (edit the words as needed & speak it confidently out loud)

I'm sticking with it! I firmly commit to keep going and push past opposition with diligence and passion. I will show up strong for those who are waiting for me. Success is near! I will stay focused on my goals - they are both meaningful and necessary.

Which Success SuperPower do you need to tap into most today? (check all that apply)

- **See Yourself Successful**
- **Shake Off Fear**
- **Do The Work**
- **Take Care of You**
- **Hold Fast To Your Faith**

What did you discover about your Success Goals?

_____

_____

_____

_____

_____

How will you *Embrace Your Power & Go* today?

_____

_____

_____

_____

_____

Just Checking In…

In Spring 1991, when I united with the Distinguished Ladies of Alpha Kappa Alpha Sorority, Inc., we memorized "Don't Quit" by Edgar A. Guest. I still know the poem by heart & recite it often to encourage myself.

"When things go wrong, as they sometimes will
When the road you're trudging seems all uphill
When the funds are low, and debts are high
And you want to smile but have to sigh
When care is pressing you down a bit
Rest, if you must, but don't you quit.

Life is queer with its twists and turns, As everyone of us sometimes learns
And many a failure turns about, When he might have won if he'd stuck it out,
Don't give up though the pace seems slow, You might succeed with another blow.

Success is failure turned inside out, The silver tint of clouds of doubt
And you never can tell how close you are
It may be near when it seems afar
So, stick to the fight when you're hardest hit
It's when things seem worst that you mustn't quit."

Success Doesn't Find You. You Must Go Get It.
(Day 23)

Pursue: for thou shalt surely overtake them, and without fail recover all.
- 1 Samuel 30:8

For some success happens by chance, others by luck, but long term, sustainable success comes by strategy.

My goal is to help you **Build a Life You Love Without Apology**. A life that is successful in every way you define success. With the right "Success Strategies" you can have it all and I want to help you succeed.

One of the biggest challenges we face as professional women is warring against the pressure to settle or even give up. We face pressure to choose or even sacrifice who we are and what we want - be it love, career, family, relationship, or lifestyle. I believe we can pursue happiness our way without compromise. We don't have to settle. There is a harmonious space where we can thrive and have it all. I'm on a mission to help you thrive.

Hear me loud and clear... Don't Settle! You *can* have it all. Now, it will take work, choices and discipline. You will need to rise to the occasion to achieve your goals. But you don't have to do it alone. Partnership is key. Enlisting experienced help is a winning strategy that helps you move ahead with intention. My clients embrace their success with strategic support. Coaching is a Game Changer. Coaching will change how you approach the Game and position you for success.

Embrace Your Power & Go!

Today's Affirmation: (edit the words as needed & speak it confidently out loud)

Today, I will pursue success in every way that I define it. I break every limiting belief that says I can't have it all. I will seek strategic support to position myself for the life I love - without apology.

Which Success SuperPower do you need to tap into most today? (check all that apply)

- **See Yourself Successful**
- **Shake Off Fear**
- **Do The Work**
- **Take Care of You**
- **Hold Fast To Your Faith**

What did you discover about your Success Goals?

_____

_____

_____

_____

_____

How will you *Embrace Your Power & Go* today?

_____

_____

_____

_____

_____

Just Checking In…

The journey to success is demanding, so please brace yourself for the ride. Many high achievers run on fumes. I know all about that. It's not often I meet people that juggle as much as I do. What every high-achiever I know as in common is the need to rest. I know because I need rest myself. I need reminders to stop and smell the roses along the way. Do you find that your work pace is so swift you sometimes forget to eat? Do you work from sunup to sundown and opt for work over enjoyment? If this sounds like you, it may just mean you need to layer in the Success SuperPower #4 "Take Care Of You" strategies. I can become so consumed when I'm all into pursuing my purpose. Once I get a glimpse of "Possible Me", I become relentless - almost to a fault. I see it more now than ever, so with intention, I am learning to pace myself, stop more often, and relax more frequently.

Self-care is a conscious act one takes in order to promote their own physical, mental, and emotional health. There are many forms that self-care may take. It could be getting enough sleep every night or stepping outside for a few minutes for fresh air. Unfortunately, many people view self-care as a luxury, rather than a priority. Consequently, they are left feeling overwhelmed, tired, and ill-equipped to handle life's inevitable challenges. When you don't take care of you, weight of chasing a dream can be crushing. Now that I know better, I do better. This is a TOP priority for me now. Make you a priority for YOU.

Old Ways Won't Open New Doors

(Day 24)

Ask and it will be given to you, seek and you will find; knock and the door will be opened to you. Matthew 7:7

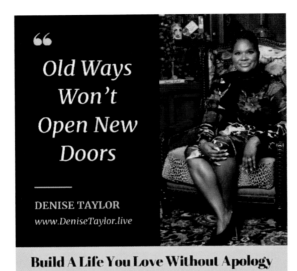

We've all heard it before and it's true: Doing the same thing and expecting different results is indeed insanity. If we want something new or different, we must be willing to do something new and different.

Life is precious and short; therefore, we must maximize every opportunity to do more, be more, have more and give more.

We must open new doors of understanding for living out our purpose, achieving our goals, and making an impact.

We must be open to new strategies, tools, resources and connections to help us grow personally, and to spark achievements in our business, career, finances and relationships.

We must open new doors to challenge self-sabotaging behavior and break negative cycles.

We must open new doors to create a personalized action plan that clearly shows the path to win.

We must open new doors to partnerships that can show us our blind spots and help us to address them.

We must open some new doors.

Build A Life You Love Without Apology.

Today's Affirmation: (edit the words as needed & speak it confidently out loud)

> Today, I put pride aside and commit to doing what works. I am more dedicated to my purpose than to any one method to achieve it. I will humble myself and accept help. I will try something new and open myself up to opportunities to learn and excel. I will open new doors.

Which Success SuperPower do you need to tap into most today? (check all that apply)

- **See Yourself Successful**
- **Shake Off Fear**
- **Do The Work**
- **Take Care of You**
- **Hold Fast To Your Faith**

What did you discover about your Success Goals?

_____

_____

_____

_____

_____

How will you *Embrace Your Power & Go* today?

_____

_____

_____

_____

_____

Just Checking In…

Heavenly Father,

I know fear comes with uncertainty. I ask that you strengthen our belief and help us to accept Your goodness above all else. Thank You for giving us power. Help us to embrace it more tightly when doubt creeps in. Thank You for guidance to chasten our mind and thoughts to what is true, honorable, right, pure, lovely, admirable, excellent, and worthy of praise. Help us shake off fear when we sense its presence and embrace our power to stand despite what we see, think, hear, or feel. Amen.

"POSSIBLE YOU"
Hold Fast To Your Faith

Many believe its luck or some sort of "hook-up" that helped the successful achieve. However, experience has shown me it really is one's ability to hold their course and keep their resolve to their vision that makes all the difference. We give up way too often and even more limiting is this notion that it will be easy. Even though "Hold Fast To Your Faith" is the last Success SuperPower, it is by far the most important. I would say it really is the key differentiator between the "Haves" and the "Have Nots" when it comes to achievement. Learning to remain in faith will revolutionize your achieving ability and track record of successes.

Vision can be so alluding, seeming distant though its close, feeling unattainable though its right in our hands and feeling foolish though its perfect. As you journey towards becoming "Possible You" you will have an incredible sense of uncertainty often and it is in those times that your faith must sustain you to stick with it.

Possible You is Possible for You.

It is the Lord who goes before you. He will be with you;
he will not leave you or forsake you. Do not fear or be dismayed.
Deuteronomy 31:8

Perhaps God never forsaking takes on hues of a "hook-up" that many assume the successful received. However, the term "hook-up" implies access that is NOT available to all - yet in this case God's help is available to everyone. Now, there is fine print… 'What you want must be in line with His Will for you." Assuming you're good on that… God can hook you up.

Knowing God is with you is comforting but **Believing God is for you** is a Game Changer.

I'll reiterate what I've already shared. Apostle I.V. Hillard is a phenomenal faith teacher. Whenever I need my faith energized, I go straight to his teachings to build my faith. He teaches when we are in faith, we have five justifiable expectations of God:
(1) We can expect God to give us a plan of action,
(2) We can expect the wisdom of God,
(3) We can expect the favor of God,
(4) We can expect a miracle from God (the supernatural to occur), and
(5) We can expect strength to endure until change comes.
I have discovered the power of holding fast to my faith which is standing in full expectation for God to show up in one or more of these ways to help me.

WHERE ARE YOU WHEN IT COMES TO YOUR FAITH?

Where does your faith need to be strengthened for "Possible You"?

We cannot get weary in pursuing God's will for us. Anything worth having is absolutely worth your pursuit, worth your diligence and worth your passion. Are you giving up when you face opposition? How is your resolve for your goals & your resolve to hold your course? Have you limited what is possible for you? In what ways do you need to build your faith?

Success SuperPower #5
Hold Fast To Your Faith

_____

_____

_____

_____

_____

_____

_____

_____

_____

_____

_____

_____

_____

_____

_____

_____

_____

_____

_____

_____

_____

_____

_____

_____

_____

_____

_____

_____

_____

_____

_____

_____

_____

_____

_____

_____

_____

_____

_____

_____

_____

_____

_____

_____

_____

_____

_____

Life, Love and the Pursuit of Happiness

EMBRACE
— YOUR POWER & —
GO!

Don't Be A Hater. It's Not A Good Look.
(Day 25)

A heart at peace gives life to the body, but envy rots the bones. - Proverbs 14:30

Envy doesn't look good on anyone! The world has abundance and there is more than enough success to go around. Once you really understand this, your career, business and your happiness will flourish.

Envy is truly more than a green-eyed monster; it is a huge distraction that will impede your progress and keep you from growing and winning. Stay focused and go BIG for your goals.

My success doesn't change your potential - just as your success doesn't change mine. Don't lose focus when you see someone else win. Success isn't a pie limited to a few slices set aside for a select and lucky few. There is plenty of success available for everyone who truly wants it. Let the wins of others serve as a reminder that it can and will happen for you, too.

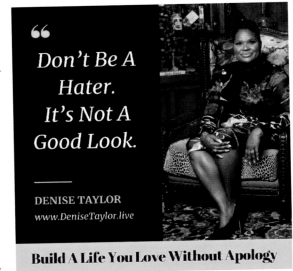

Embrace Your Power & Go!

Today's Affirmation: (edit the words as needed & speak it confidently out loud)

I am a WINNER. True winners are anchored in purpose and security. True winners focus on their own blessings while celebrating the victories of others. The world is abundant. There is more than enough success for everyone. There is more than enough success for me.

Which Success SuperPower do you need to tap into most today? (check all that apply)

- **See Yourself Successful**
- **Shake Off Fear**
- **Do The Work**
- **Take Care of You**
- **Hold Fast To Your Faith**

What did you discover about your Success Goals?

_____

_____

_____

_____

_____

How will you *Embrace Your Power & Go* today?

_____

_____

_____

_____

_____

Begin With Gratefulness

(Day 26)

Enter into his gates with thanksgiving and into his courts with praise ... - Psalm 100:4

Once you understand how blessed you truly are, you will be far less anxious and way more grateful. Having a grateful heart brings on an authentic perspective that settles your soul. You begin to see things differently. You're able to think with clarity and wisdom.

While I have learned to be content, I still refuse to settle. And while I have learned to seek what I desire, I do it knowing I am already blessed. I am grateful and I choose to start from there. This ensures that whatever I face, I am secure because I started from a place of gratitude.

Start each day by reflecting on your blessings. Write down three things that you're grateful for each morning. This will allow you to focus on goodness and shift your thinking in a powerful way.

Be grateful...

Today's Affirmation: (edit the words as needed & speak it confidently out loud)

I choose to begin each day from a place of gratitude. I know that I am blessed, and I will carry this mindset with me throughout my day. I am confidently secure because the Creator of the whole world and every galaxy in the universe inhabits my praises.

Which Success SuperPower do you need to tap into most today? (check all that apply)

- **See Yourself Successful**
- **Shake Off Fear**
- **Do The Work**
- **Take Care of You**
- **Hold Fast To Your Faith**

What did you discover about your Success Goals?

_____

_____

_____

_____

_____

How will you _Embrace Your Power & Go_ today?

_____

_____

_____

_____

_____

Just checking in…

"One of the best signs of growth is seeing yourself no longer worried, bothered or hurt by the things that once drained you. You're better, stronger, wiser - and it feels so good." - Idil Ahmed

You know what I love? I love the fact that God has given me this insatiable appetite to be the very best I can. Settling just gives me the creeps and turns my stomach. I've got a real BIG God on my side, and I am not ashamed to GO BIG!!! #turndownforwhat

"Prayers are the best predictors of your spiritual future. Who you become is determined by how you pray. The transcript of your prayers becomes the script of your life." - Mark Batterson

"If your prayers aren't impossible to you, they are insulting God. Why? Because they don't require divine intervention. God is moved to omnipotent action." – Mark Batterson

Two things define you - your patience when you have nothing and your attitude when you have everything. – Imam Ali

Tell me, just what are the transcripts of your prayers? Do they indicate Power or pity?

Don't Wait For Opportunity. Create It.
(Day 27)

I. wisdom, dwell with prudence, and find out knowledge of witty inventions.
- Proverbs 8:12

Your ideas are incredible so don't discount them. Allow them to flourish and come alive. We mistakenly pick apart the divine downloads we receive and often reason them away. Instead, we should be inspired to try, inspired to create, inspired to believe.

We are empowered by God to create, and yet we too often find ourselves waiting in the wings for someone or something to affirm our inspiration. You have everything you need to get started.

I've discovered that God gives you more on the way than He does at the start. He wants to see your faith in action. Always remember creativity is your birthright as a child of the Creator. You were born to make things happen.

Embrace Your Power & Go!

Today's Affirmation: (edit the words as needed & speak it confidently out loud)

I was born to create. Creativity is my birthright as the child of the ultimate Creator. I am a Destiny Designer as I create opportunities for myself and others every day. Problem-solving is in my DNA.

Which Success SuperPower do you need to tap into most today? (check all that apply)

- **See Yourself Successful**
- **Shake Off Fear**
- **Do The Work**
- **Take Care of You**
- **Hold Fast To Your Faith**

What did you discover about your Success Goals?

_____

_____

_____

_____

_____

How will you _Embrace Your Power & Go_ today?

_____

_____

_____

_____

_____

Just Checking In…

I love Bishop T.D. Jakes. Truth is … he mentored me from a distance.

I'd wake up early and spend focused time devouring every teaching of his that I could get my hands on. It was Bishop Jakes who helped me get loosed from all of the things that happened to me in my childhood. His messages pushed me to embrace my power.

I marvel at his success. He shows up so dynamically - across the board - in unexpected spaces, leveraging every talent, gift and interest God blessed him to have. For instance: He oversees a global mega church; preaches nearly every Sunday; pastors other pastors; writes plays and directs movies; hosts three marquee conference brands, writes bestselling books, sings, produces music, and plays the piano; advocates for the incarcerated and serves as an International Humanitarian… I rattled those accolades off in just 10 seconds, but the truth is, he is way more and does way more than just those things. What he does the best and what I truly admire most … he is creating a legacy for his family.

I am also amazed how no one bats an eye at ALL he does. Yet, what I often hear of my own work and accomplishments is "You're doing so much." I agree. I am doing a lot. And while I am learning to rest … please don't expect me to stop. My mentor, Bishop Jakes, showed me what is possible when you simply seek to serve ONE. And I'm after all the ONEs I can get.

Don't Be Afraid Of Going Slow.
Be Afraid Of Standing Still.
(Day 28)

The race is not given to the swift, nor the battle to the strong ... Ecclesiastes 9:11

Remind yourself often to "Keep Moving Forward!"

Whatever your goals, keep going. Whatever your aspirations, keep going. Whatever your dreams, keep going. Anything worth having or achieving, is indeed worth your diligence.

Success is not eluding you; the pursuit is maturing you. Growth and experience are worth gold. Don't sidestep the process - for it is the process that prepares you for the next level.

Fix your focus, steady your attitude, and keep moving forward. Dream Big and Finish Strong. Get help if you need it. But don't you stop.

Embrace Your Power & Go!

Today's Affirmation: (edit the words as needed & speak it confidently out loud)

Today, I will patiently embrace the process that is required to achieve my dreams. I will resist the temptation to speed past necessary steps and give my vision the time and diligence it deserves. Though I may pause to recalibrate many times along my journey, I refuse to stop.

Which Success SuperPower do you need to tap into most today? (check all that apply)

- **See Yourself Successful**
- **Shake Off Fear**
- **Do The Work**
- **Take Care of You**
- **Hold Fast To Your Faith**

What did you discover about your Success Goals?

_____

_____

_____

_____

_____

How will you _Embrace Your Power & Go_ today?

_____

_____

_____

_____

_____

Just Checking In…

Disney nailed it - KEEP MOVING FORWARD!!!

I can think of so many times in every aspect of my life when I felt like things were not going to work out. Be it in Life, Love, or Happiness … I often had to pick up pieces. I can say today, I am so glad I stooped down and picked up what was left. I took those handfuls, and I am winning.

Embracing the Success SuperPowers has equipped me to chase purpose with power. I've faced many situations, circumstances, and conditions that seemed greater than what I had left in my hand - yet God always made a way for me to triumph. He nurtured my mind to trust Him, boosting my commitment, consistency, and confidence to build a life I love.

See Yourself Successful
Shake Off Fear
Do The Work
Take Care Of You
Hold Fast To Your Faith
These are Gamechangers!

I stand by these SuperPowers to change your life. They have indeed changed mine.

Focus On Your Goals – Not Your Obstacles

(Day 29)

I'm doing a great work; I can't come down. - Nehemiah 6:3

It's really easy to get distracted, to decrease, or even lose our intensity. We can become overwhelmed and before we know it, we have let minor distractions take center stage, disrupting our pursuit.

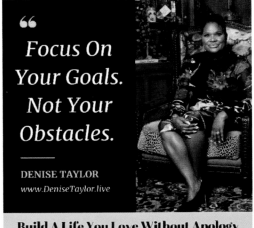

Focus means diligent concentration on the priority. Distractions are going to come, but we must overcome the urge to give them more attention than they deserve. Nothing should stop our pursuit. We may slow down, but we should never stop. The power is in our hands to be, do, or have what we desire.

"Because the Sovereign LORD helps me, I will not be disgraced. Therefore, have I set my face like flint, and I know I will not be put to shame" (Isaiah 50:7).

We must set our face (focus) like a hard immovable rock when it comes to our purpose. We must demonstrate unwavering determination, diligence, and perseverance. Good news! Help is available. We have an enduring promise from God that if we set our focus … "We will not be put to shame". Now that's where it gets sweet … Woot, there it is.

Embrace Your Power & Go!

Today's Affirmation: (edit the words as needed & speak it confidently out loud)

Distractions don't have a chance, today. With determination, diligence, and unwavering perseverance, I have set my focus. I am secure in the promise that my Sovereign Lord will help me and that I will not be put to shame. I will get what I showed up for!

Which Success SuperPower do you need to tap into most today? (check all that apply)

- **See Yourself Successful**
- **Shake Off Fear**
- **Do The Work**
- **Take Care of You**
- **Hold Fast To Your Faith**

What did you discover about your Success Goals?

_____

_____

_____

_____

_____

How will you *Embrace Your Power & Go* today?

_____

_____

_____

_____

_____

Believe in Yourself.

Delay Is Not Denial

(Day 30)

For still the vision awaits its appointed time … If it seems slow, wait for it; it will surely come … Habakkuk 2:3

I love quotes, phrases and sayings because they serve as reminders and succinctly sum up my thoughts. The classic and witty saying, "Delay is not Denial" is one on my favs because it is a reminder to not only trust the process, but to stay prepared for the expected end. Now, that's good!

We have to be mindful that the only thing standing between our dream and the realization of our dream is time. That's all. Just time. And to that point, everything is "just a matter of time." During that "time" we are afforded the opportunity to do the one thing that God requires most from us - to trust Him.

You see, there are truths that we can rest in while we wait.

(1) His promises are sure (2 Corinthians 1:20).

(2) He has a plan for us that is good (Jeremiah 29:11)

(3) He is always with us (Hebrews 13:5)

When we meditate on these promises, we are not distracted or discouraged by delay. It is just a matter of timing for our vision and God's plan to become full. He is always working everything out for our good. Always.

We must SEE things differently. We must SEE God at work.

It's coming. Just believe.

Embrace Your Power & Go!

Today's Affirmation: (edit the words as needed & speak it confidently out loud)

Faith waits. I will wait patiently but with great expectation as I meditate on the promises of God. I have a good Heavenly Father who doesn't play games with my heart. He is faithful. I will see the fulfillment of everything He promised.

Which Success SuperPower do you need to tap into most today? (check all that apply)

- **See Yourself Successful**
- **Shake Off Fear**
- **Do The Work**
- **Take Care of You**
- **Hold Fast To Your Faith**

What did you discover about your Success Goals?

_____

_____

_____

_____

_____

How will you *Embrace Your Power & Go* today?

_____

_____

_____

_____

_____

Just Checking In...

My Prayer For You

Heavenly Father,

*Thank you for this shared journey over the last 30 days. I stand in full expectation that greatness will manifest with abundance in their life. I look forward to praise reports of their success. All glory and honor that shines our way belongs to them. I pray diligence in the life of the one who has finished this journey. Continue to shine supernaturally in their lives so they can **Embrace Their Power & Go!** Thank You for Your grace and mercy. May it always continue to abound richly in their lives. Lord, please strengthen them to hold fast to their faith. In Jesus' Name. Amen.*

"POSSIBLE YOU"?
It's Time To Soar

Throughout this journey you have discovered more about "Possible You"

Possible You is Possible for You.

What clarity have you gained through this experience about becoming "Possible You"?

The Finale is simple:
Your challenge is to truly Embrace Your Power and Be, Do, Have and Achieve "Possible You"

'For I know the plans I have for you,' declares the Lord, 'plans to prosper you and not to harm you, plans to give you a hope and a future.
Jeremiah 29:11

Begin with that promise as the foundation and outline your next steps.

_____

_____

_____

_____

_____

_____

_____

_____

_____

_____

_____

_____

_____

_____

_____

_____

_____

_____

_____

_____

_____

_____

_____

_____

_____

_____

_____

_____

_____

_____

_____

_____

_____

_____

_____

_____

Life, Love and the Pursuit of Happiness

EMBRACE
— YOUR POWER & —
GO!

_____

_____

_____

_____

_____

_____

_____

_____

_____

_____

_____

_____

_____

_____

_____

_____

_____

_____

_____

_____

_____

_____

_____

_____

_____

_____

Life, Love and the Pursuit of Happiness

EMBRACE
— YOUR POWER & —
GO!

Life, Love and the Pursuit of Happiness

EMBRACE
— YOUR POWER & —
GO!

Made in the USA
Middletown, DE
25 August 2022

ELEONORA KIRPICHNIKOVA

RUSSIAN GRAMMAR: FORM AND FUNCTION 1

ИМЕНИТЕЛЬНЫЙ ПАДЕЖ NOMINATIVE CASE

SINGULAR

	Окончания (endings)	Примеры (examples)
		Именительный падеж (Nominative case)
Мужской род (masculine)	consonant - й - ь	стол, паспорт, компьютер, телефон музей, чай секретарь, шампунь, гость
Женский род (feminine)	- а - я - ь	библиотека, виза, фирма деревня, фамилия площадь, мать
Средний род (neuter)	- о - е - мя	яблоко, метро, письмо море, поле время, имя

Exceptions – masculine	
папа	мужчина
дядя	кофе
дедушка	

Exercise 1

Собака, профессия, чай, музей, мать, дедушка, окно, море, журнал, город, карандаш, машина, друг, подруга, время, банк, фамилия, врач, кошка, черепаха, бабушка, книга, стол, интернет, дерево, дочь, папа, сын, кот, утка, огурец.

он

она

оно

Exercise 2

Кот, кошка, птица, сова, пингвин, собака, яблоко, яйцо, рыба, лимон, ананас, клубника, круассан, чай, сыр, ложка, виноград, кукуруза, вода, кофе.

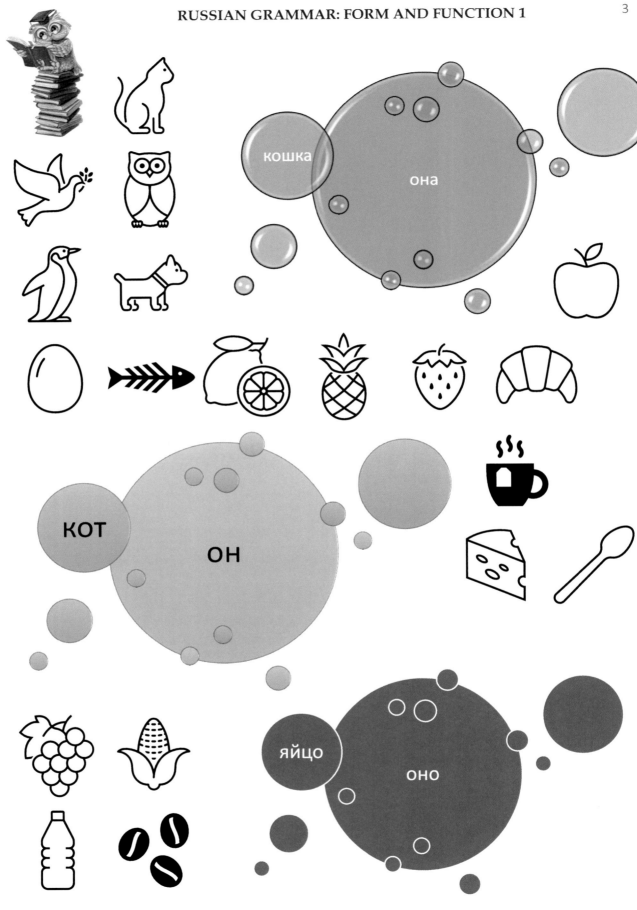

PLURAL

	Окончания (endings)	Примеры (examples)	
		Именительный падеж (Nominative case/SINGULAR)	Именительный падеж (Nominative case/PLURAL)
Мужской род (masculine)	cons. + ы й, ь → и	Это стол. Это словарь.	Это столы. Это словари.
Женский род (feminine)	а → ы я, ь → и	Это машина. Это площадь.	Это машины. Это площади.
Средний род (neuter)	о → а е → я мя → мена	Это окно. Это поле. Это имя.	Это окна. Это поля. Это имена.

Exceptions 1

мать – матери
дочь – дочери
сын – сыновья
сестра -сёстры
брат – братья
друг – друзья
город – города

такси – такси
метро – метро
кофе – кофе
пальто – пальто
пианино – пианино
манго – манго
киви – киви

лес – леса
вечер – вечера
поезд – поезда
паспорт - паспорта
дом – дома
ребёнок -дети
человек – люди
дерево – деревья
стул – стулья
яблоко – яблоки
учитель - учителя

видео – видео
граффити – граффити
спагетти - спагетти

 **Ы→И after «Г, К, Х, Ж, Ч, Ш, Щ»**

Мы подруги. Это книги. В этом городе есть библиотеки. Мы врачи. Это карандаши.

Exceptions 2	ALWAYS PLURAL

деньги
часы
брюки
штаны
ножницы
джинсы
очки

 Exercise 3

1.   Врач - врачи
2. Имя – ....
3. Друг – ....

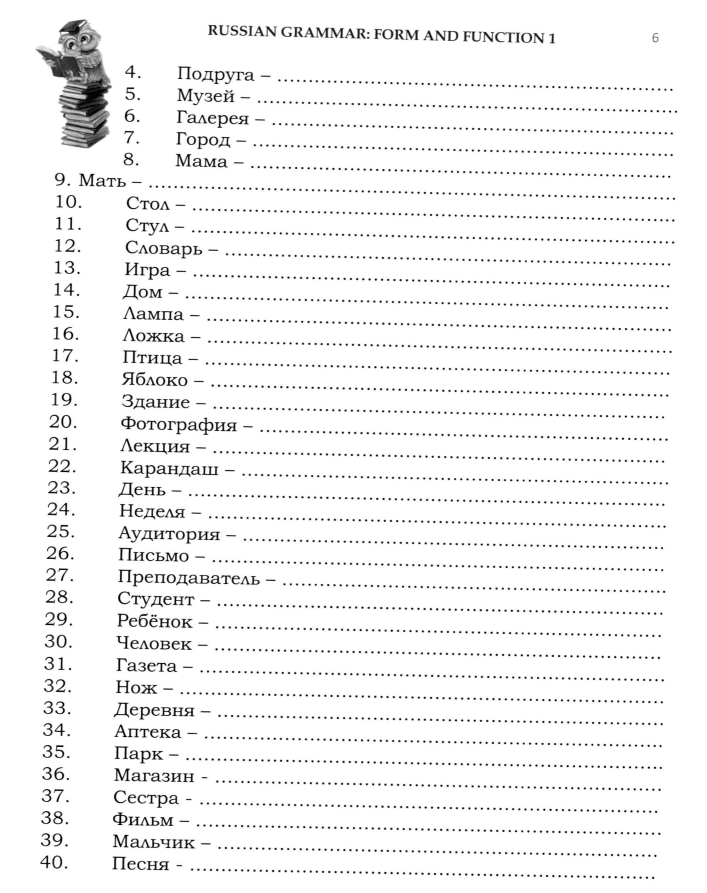

4.   Подруга – ....

5.   Музей – ....

6.   Галерея – ....

7.   Город – ....

8.   Мама – ....

9. Мать – ....

10.   Стол – ....

11.   Стул – ....

12.   Словарь – ....

13.   Игра – ....

14.   Дом – ....

15.   Лампа – ....

16.   Ложка – ....

17.   Птица – ....

18.   Яблоко – ....

19.   Здание – ....

20.   Фотография – ....

21.   Лекция – ....

22.   Карандаш – ....

23.   День – ....

24.   Неделя – ....

25.   Аудитория – ....

26.   Письмо – ....

27.   Преподаватель – ....

28.   Студент – ....

29.   Ребёнок – ....

30.   Человек – ....

31.   Газета – ....

32.   Нож – ....

33.   Деревня – ....

34.   Аптека – ....

35.   Парк – ....

36.   Магазин - ....

37.   Сестра - ....

38.   Фильм – ....

39.   Мальчик – ....

40.   Песня - ....

Exercise 4

Что это? Кто это?

Exercise 5

Что Вы видите?

он	она	оно
стол	картина	окно

ПРЕДЛОЖНЫЙ ПАДЕЖ PREPOSITIONAL CASE

SINGULAR

	Окончания (endings)	Примеры (examples)	
		Именительный падеж (Nominative case)	Предложный падеж (Prepositional case)
Мужской род (masculine)	cons.+ е й →е ь→е ий→ии	Это стол. Это музей. Это секретарь. Это санаторий.	Книга на столе. Она работает в музее. Он говорит о секретаре. Они отдыхают в санатории.
Женский род (feminine)	а→е я→е ь→и ия→ии	Это библиотека. Это деревня. Это площадь. Это Италия.	Она читает в библиотеке. Бабушка живёт в деревне. Памятник на площади. Они живут в Италии.
Средний род (neuter)	о→е е→е ие→ии	Это метро. Это море. Это здание.	Он едет на метро. Она мечтает о море. В задании есть лифт.

PREPOSITIONAL CASE FUNCTIONS:

- **LOCATION**

Я живу в деревне. Она читает в библиотеке. Они обедают в кафе.

- **MONTHS OF THE YEAR**

Я была в Вашингтоне в марте.

- **TALK/THINK/DREAM/ASK/WRITE/READ etc. ABOUT**

Я думаю о сестре. Он рассказывает о фильме. Они читают о России.

- **TRANSPORT**

Я езжу на машине. Я не люблю ездить на автобусе.

- **PLAYING MUSICAL INSTRUMENTS**

Моя мама играет на рояле. Мой друг играет на гитаре.

– Где Вы работаете?

– Я работаю **в магазине**.

– Это работа Вашей мечты?

– Нет, я мечтаю **о музыке**.

– Вы играете **на гитаре**?

– Нет, я играю **на пианино**.

– А на чём Вы ездите?

– Я езжу **на машине**.

– А где стоит Ваша машина?

– Она стоит **в гараже**.

– А что Вы делаете **в октябре**?

– Я обычно работаю **в октябре**.

в декабре   в марте
в январе   в апреле
в феврале   в мае

в июне   в сентябре
в июле   в октябре
в августе   в ноябре

Он живёт в городе.

Цветы стоят в вазе.

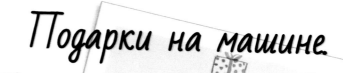

Подарки на машине.

Кот мечтает о рыбе.

Девочка играет на скрипке.

Он едет на автобусе.

Exercise 1

1.   Где ты живёшь? – Я живу в .... (Вашингтон).

2. Моя сестра работает в .... (библиотека).

3. В .... (август) я был в .... (Италия)

4. Дети играют на .... (улица).

5. Мой брат учится в .... (университет).

6. Ты хочешь жить в .... (Россия)?

7. Где мой словарь? – Он лежит на .... (стол).

8. Вчера мы ужинали во французском .... (ресторан).

9. Ты часто бегаешь в .... (парк)?

10.   Мой папа – посол. Он работает в .... (посольство).

11.   Во .... (Владивосток) хорошая погода в .... (август и сентябрь (м.р.).

12.   Я часто отдыхаю в .... (Испания и Греция).

13.   Она секретарь, она работает в .... (офис).

14.   Моя подруга живёт в .... (Германия).

15.   Где Лувр? – Лувр в .... (Париж).

16.   Где Кремль? – Кремль в .... (Москва).

17.   Где живут кенгуру? – Кенгуру живут в .... (Австралия).

18.   Мы вчера были в .... (зоопарк).

19.   Он всегда много рассказывает о .... (семья).

20.   Я часто езжу на работу на .... (автобус).

в марте,
в апреле,
в мае

в декабре,
в январе,
в феврале

в июне,
в июле,
в августе

Exercise 2

Привет! Меня зовут Анна. Я люблю путешествовать.

В .... (декабрь (м.р.) я была в .... (Япония).

В .... (март) я была в ....(Лондон).

В ....
(апрель (м.р.) я
была в ....(Прага).

В .... (июнь (м.р.) я была в .... (Ирландия).

В .... (сентябрь (м.р.) я была в .... (Финляндия).

Exercise 3

1. Где ноутбук? – Ноутбук на столе.

2. Где очки? – ....

3. Где книги? -...................

4. Где машина? - ....

5. Где мужчина? - ....

6. Где яблоко? - ....

7. Где собака? - ....

8. Где девочка? -

....

В

- внутри (в здании, в доме, в комнате, в коробке, в школе, в кафе, в университете)
- в космосе
- в мире
- в стране, городе, деревне, штате, районе
- в воде: в океане, в море, в реке
- в Интернете, в чате, в "Фейсбуке"

В +location	На+event/surface
в библиотеке	на концерте
в деревне	на уроке
в России	на совещании
в театре	на экзамене
в магазине	на встрече
в университете	на выставке
в городе	на балете
в стране	на вечеринке
в доме	на стене
в здании	на столе

на

- на поверхности (на столе, на полке)
- снаружи: на улице, на площади, на стадионе, на рынке, на проспекте
- на платене, на континенте, на острове, на горе, на севере, на востоке, на юге, на западе
- рядом с водой: на море, на озере
- событие: на работе, на экскурсии, на лекции, на операции, на собрании
- структура: на курсе, на факультете
- на сайте, на странице, на форуме

Пальмы на острове.
Остров в океане.

Подарок в коробке.

Цветы в вазе. Ваза на столе.

Картина на стене. Ковёр на полу.
Лампа в углу. Плед на диване.

Космонавт в космосе. Он на
работе.

Exercise 4

Где плавает черепаха? - ....

Где отдыхает девушка? - ....

Где лодка? - ....

Где собор? - ....

Где они играют? - ....

Где студенты? - ....

Exceptions 1

в горах	на острове
в отпуске	на родине
в экспедиции	на юге
в командировке	на севере
на фабрике	на западе
на заводе	на востоке
на почте	на стадионе
на вокзале	на даче
на рынке	на площади
на улице	на ферме

Exceptions 2

в шкафу	на берегу
в углу	на мосту
на полу	в порту
в саду	в аэропорту
в Крыму	на метро
в лесу	на пианино

Exceptions 3

дочь – дочери	матери - матерях
мать – матери	друзья – друзьях
	сыновья – сыновьях
	дочери- дочерях
	братья – братьях
	отцы – отцах
	люди – людях
	дети - детях

думать о, говорить о

читать о, рассказывать о

писать о

мечтать о

спрашивать о, спорить о

помнить о, вспоминать о

Exercise 5

О чём он говорит? - ....

О чём они говорят? - ....

О чём они говорят? - ....

О чём она думает? - ....

О чём она мечтает? - ....

О чём он читает? - ....

Exercise 6

В/НА?

1. Говорят, что .... Марсе была жизнь.
2. Вчера мы были .... балете.
3. Мой папа работает .... фабрике.
4. Они живут .... Аргентине.
5. Мальчики играют в футбол ....стадионе.
6. Я никогда не была .... севере России.
7. Я работаю .... библиотеке.

8.   Мой сын учится ………. университете.
9.   Ребёнок играет ……….полу.
10.   В прошлом году мы отдыхали ………. Крыму ……….
море.
11.   Я так давно не был ………. театре!
12.   ………. аэропорту было очень много туристов.
13.   Диван стоит ………. углу.
14.   Я учусь ………. университете, ………. филологическом
факультете.
15.   ………. улице идёт дождь.
16.   Я всегда покупаю овощи ………. рынке.
17.   Что ты обычно делаешь ………. даче? – Я работаю
………. саду.
18.   Почему ты сидишь ………. полу?
19.   Моя мама работает ………. почте.
20.   Вчера я очень устал ………. работе.

Exercise 7

1.   Где говорят по-английски?
2. Где очень тепло? А где очень холодно?
3. Где Вы покупаете фрукты?
4. Где Вы любите гулять?
5. Где работает Ваша мама?
6. Где Вы учитесь?
7. О Чём Вы мечтаете?
8. О чём Вы любите читать?
9. Где модно играть в футбол?
10.   Где можно слушать джаз?
11.   На чём Вы ездите на работу?
12.   Вы были вчера в театре?
13.   Вы живёте в России?
14.   Где Вы любите ужинать?
15.   Где находится Прага?
16.   Кто был на Луне?
17.   Вы уже были в Санкт-Петербурге?
18.   Ваш папа работает в школе?

19.   Вы были на почте на прошлой неделе?
20.   Вы были на море в этом году?
21.   Вы купались в море в этом году?
22.   Вы были на Кубе?
23.   О чём говорят бизнесмены?
24.   О чём говорят политики?
25.   О ком Вы часто думаете?
26.   Ваш дом в Москве?
27.   Где живут японцы?
28.   Вы когда-нибудь отдыхали на Тенерифе?
29.   О чём Вы читаете в Интернете?
30.   Что Вы обычно делаете в парке?

PLURAL

	Окончания (endings)	Примеры (examples)	
		Именительный падеж (Nominative case) (singular)	Предложный падеж (Prepositional case) (plural)
Множественное число (plural)	cons., а, о→ах	Это библиотека.	Студенты читают в библиотеках.
	й, ь, е, я →ях	Это словарь.	Он смотрит слова в словарях.

Exercise 8

1. Люди живут в .... (города).
2. Студенты учатся в .... (университеты).
3. Я рассказываю о .... (братья).

4.   Бабушка любит говорить о .... (внуки).
5.   Информацию можно найти в .... (книги).
6.   Я должен подумать о .... (слова) мамы.
7.   Я не люблю говорить о .... (фильмы).
8.   В .... (страны) Европы все говорят на нескольких языках.
9. Я думаю о .... (проблемы).
10.   Они ужинают в .... (рестораны).

Exercise 9

Где они?

ВИНИТЕЛЬНЫЙ ПАДЕЖ ACCUSATIVE CASE

SINGULAR

	Окончания (endings)		Примеры (examples)	
			Именительный падеж (Nominative case)	Винительный падеж (Accusative case)
Мужской род (masculine)	animate	cons.+ а ь→я	Это студент. Это учитель.	Она видит студента. Она любит учителя.
	inanimate	Accusative = Nominative	Это салат. Это словарь.	Я хочу салат. Я покупаю словарь.
Женский род (feminine)		а→у я→ю ь→ь	Это библиотека. Это деревня. Это площадь.	Она видит библиотеку. Бабушка любит деревню. Я вижу площадь.
Средний род (neuter)		Accusative = Nominative	Это метро. Это море.	Она не любит метро. Он любит море.

ACCUSATIVE CASE FUNCTIONS:

- ## DIRECT OBJECT

Я хочу салат. Бабушка любит внука. Я читаю книгу.

- ## DIRECTION OF MOVEMENT (WHERE TO?)

Я хожу в школу каждый день. Я иду на почту.

- ## DAYS OF THE WEEK

  - в понедельник

  - во вторник

  - в среду

  - в четверг

  - в пятницу

  - в субботу

  - в воскресенье

- ## GAMES AND SPORTS

Дети играют в теннис. Я играю в футбол. Друзья играют в баскетбол.

Я учусь в школе. Я работаю в библиотеке. (Prepositional case) /статика – где?/

Я хожу в школу. Я иду в библиотеку. (Accusative case) /движение – куда?/

Я хочу десерт.

Аня ходит в школу каждый день.

Моя мама любит
тюльпаны.

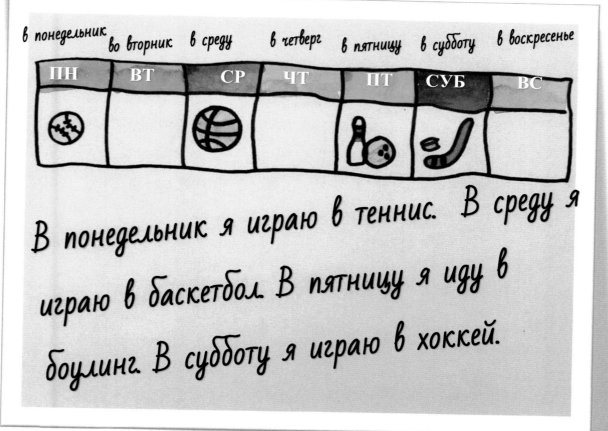

В понедельник я играю в теннис. В среду я играю в баскетбол. В пятницу я иду в боулинг. В субботу я играю в хоккей.

Exercise 1

1. Бабушка читает .... (книга).

2. Я покупаю .... (хлеб) и .... (курица).

3. Мы смотрим интересный .... (фильм).

4. Я люблю .... (молоко).

5. Я хочу .... (паста) и .... (сок).

6. Я не слушаю .... (рок), я слушаю .... (классика).

7. Я изучаю .... (генетика).

8. Ты хочешь .... (кофе)?

9. Что ты читаешь? – Я читаю .... (детектив).

10. Моя мама никогда не смотрит .... (реклама).

11. В .... (суббота) я играю в .... (футбол) с друзьями.

12. В .... (пятница) я иду в .... (театр).

13. Сегодня мы идём в .... (ресторан).

14. Вчера мы были на выставке, а сегодня идём на .... (опера).

15. Куда Вы идёте в .... (понедельник)? – Мы идём в .... (музей).

Exercise 2

Собака любит ……………… (кошка).

Попугай не любит ……………… (кошка).

Они любят ……………… (рыбалка).

Она купила ……………… (матрёшка).

Она слушает .... (музыка).

Он читает .... (газета).

Они продали .... (дом).

Exercise 3

Это Ася. Она – шопоголик. Что Ася купила на этой неделе?

Пример. В понедельник Ася купила юбку.

понедельник	юбка
вторник	платье
среда	блузка
четверг	сумка
пятница	сувенир
суббота	картина
воскресенье	календарь

Exercise 4

Это Андрей и Марина. Они не любят сидеть дома. Куда они ездили/ходили на этой неделе?

Пример. В понедельник они ездили на пляж.

понедельник	пляж
вторник	библиотека
среда	ресторан
четверг	кафе
пятница	театр
суббота	галерея
воскресенье	деревня

PLURAL

	Окончания (endings)	Примеры (examples)	
		Именительный падеж (Nominative case) (singular)	Винительный падеж (Accusative case) (plural)
Множественное число (plural) ANIMATE	cons.+ ов/ей ь, я →ей/ь й→ев а→_/ек/ок	Это врач. Это студент. Это учитель. Это герой. Это студентка.	Я вижу врачей. Я вижу студентов. Я слушаю учителей. Я встретил героев. Я вижу студенток.
Множественное число (plural) INANIMATE	Accusative = Nominative	Это книга. Это журнал.	Я покупаю книги. Я читаю журналы.

Это кошка. Я люблю кош**е**к. [о/е after "ш/щ/ч/ж"]

Это студентка. Я вижу студент**о**к.

Exceptions

матери – матерей   братья-братьев
дети-детей
дочери – дочерей
сёстры-сестёр
сыновья -сыновей
друзья – друзей
люди-людей
врач - врачей

Exercise 5

1.   Что Вы читаете вечером?
2. Что Вы сейчас видите?
3. Что Вы покупаете в супермаркете?
4. Что Вы едите на обед?
5. Что Вы любите пить утром?
6. Что Вы пишите на работе?
7. Что Вы сейчас изучаете?
8. Что Вы слушаете в машине?
9. Что Вы любите рассказывать?
10.   Какой фрукт Вам нравится?
11.   В какой день Вы встаёте рано?
12.   В какой день Вы встаёте поздно?
13.   Куда Вы едете в ноябре?
14.   Куда идёт врач?
15.   Вы любите играть в футбол? А шахматы? В баскетбол?
16.   Когда Вы идёте на балет?
17.   Где Вы были в воскресенье?
18.   Как часто Вы ходите в театр?
19.   Какой овощ Вы не любите?
20.   Какой Ваш любимый фильм?

21. Вы любите рыбу или курицу?
22. Что спрашивает преподаватель?
23. Кого Вы видели вчера?
24. Куда ходят дети каждый день?
25. Вы пишите письма?
26. Как часто Вы ходите на работу?
27. Что Вы можете нарисовать?
28. Вы пишите письма?
29. Что любит Ваша мама?
30. Когда Вы делаете домашнее задание по русскому языку?

Exercise 6

Это Максим. Он блогер-путешественник. Посмотрите на фотографии и расскажите, когда и куда Максим поедет в этом году.

Пример. В августе Максим едет в Норвегию.

Март/Германия

Декабрь/Италия

Сентябрь/Индонезия

Апрель/Мексика

А куда Вы едете/летите в этом году?

Exercise 7

1. Я готовлю (салат, пицца, суп, лазанья, десерт, мясо, рыба).
2. Я слушаю (новости, радио, музыка, концерт, опера, интервью).
3. Я играю в (футбол, баскетбол, гольф, волейбол, шахматы, хоккей).
4. Я хожу в (библиотека, магазин, парк, ресторан, театр).
5. Я хожу на (работа, балет, опера, ужин, концерт).
6. Я читаю (книга, журнал, газета, статья, письмо).
7. Я пишу (письмо, блог, отчёт, стихотворение).
8. Я смотрю (фильм, новости, телевизор, сериал, детектив).
9. Я люблю (фрукты, вино, чай, сыр, мороженое, шоколад).
10. Я ненавижу (брокколи, капуста, майонез, бутерброды).

Exercise 8

Куда муж и жена идут вечером?

Куда сегодня идёт студент?

Куда они идут сегодня вечером?

Куда мы идём завтра?

Exercise 8

Что Вы видите?

ДАТЕЛЬНЫЙ ПАДЕЖ DATIVE CASE

SINGULAR

	Окончания (endings)	Примеры (examples)	
		Именительный падеж (Nominative case)	Дательный падеж (Dative case)
Мужской род (masculine)	cons.+ у й, ь→ю	Это сын. Это друг. Это учитель. Это писатель.	Сыну 7 лет. Я звоню другу. Учителю 40 лет. Я помогаю писателю.
Женский род (feminine)	а→е я→е ь→и ия→ии	Это мама. Это Оля. Это площадь. Это Мария.	Маме 30 лет. Я звоню Оле. Площади 100 лет. Я помогаю Марии.
Средний род (neuter)	о→у е→ю ие→ию	Это письмо. Это море. Это здание.	Я рада письму. Морю много лет. Зданию 15 лет.

DATIVE CASE FUNCTIONS:

- ### INDIRECT OBJECT

Я дарю подарок маме. Он звонит другу. Бабушка рассказывает историю внучке.

- ## AGE

Папе 40 лет. Девочке 5 лет.

WITH PREPOSITIONS:	
ПО	Я врач **по профессии**. Я русский **по национальности**. Я слушаю новости **по радио**. Я смотрю фильм **по телевизору**. Это мне прислали **по почте**. Сегодня лекция по физике. Это учебник по русскому языку. Завтра экзамен по литературе. Я гуляю по парку. Я хожу по магазинам.
К (when you go to see a person)	Я иду к другу. Я иду к врачу. Я еду к родителям.

VERBS WHICH REQUIRE DATIVE	
нравиться	Подруге нравится эта книга.
давать	Коллеге дали зарплату.

говорить	Папа говорит сыну сделать уроки.
рекомендовать	Он рекомендовал туристам этот отель.
дарить	Дети подарили маме открытку.
звонить	Я часто звоню подруге.
помогать	Он всегда помогает другу.
рассказывать	Актёр рассказал журналисту интересную историю.
советовать	Мама всегда советует детям, что нужно делать.
объяснять	Учитель объясняет ученикам дательный падеж.
обещать	Муж пообещал жене поездку в Италию.

показывать	Риелтор показал клиентам новый дом.
писать	Бабушка пишет письмо подруге.
покупать	Он купил маме цветы.

- **НЕЛЬЗЯ/МОЖНО/НУЖНО**

Детям нужно есть фрукты. Детям нельзя есть много шоколада.

- **FEELINGS/CONDITION (DAT.+ADVERB):**

Бабушке холодно. Папе жарко. Студентам интересно смотреть фильм. Детям весело играть на улице. Студентам трудно говорить по-русски.

Мы были в музее. - Мы ходили по музею целый час.

Я был в парке. - Я гулял по парку два часа.

Она врач по профессии.

- Кто ты по национальности?

- Я русская.

По радио играет музыка.

Туристам нравится звёздное небо.

Снеговику жарко.

Детям нельзя есть много сладкого.

Риелтор показал клиентам маленький домик.

Врач советует пациенту пить зелёный чай.

Бабушке нравится мёд.

Городу 800 лет.

Мама объясняет сыну, что в лимоне много витамина С.

Exercise 1

1. Папа дарит цветы .... (мама).

2. Врач помогает .... (пациент).

3. (Дедушка) .... холодно.

4. (Бабушка) .... неинтересно играть в компьютерные игры.

5. Аня и Оля гуляют по .... (парк).

6. Мой муж – инженер по .... (профессия).

7. Вы часто слушаете новости по .... (радио).

8. Вы покупаете шоколад .... (сын)?

9. Что Вы дарите .... (жена) на день рождения?

10. Вы плохо выглядите, Вы должны идти к .... (врач).

11. Туристы гуляют по .... (город).

12. (Кошка) .... нравится играть.

13. (Турист) .... нравится Красная площадь.

14. (Дедушка) .... нравится исторический музей.

15. Моя мама каждый день разговаривает по .... (телефон).

16. Моя подруга американка по .... (национальность).

17. (Писатель) .... нужна бумага.

18. Студенты обещают ....(преподаватель) хорошо учиться.

19. Я верю .... (президент).

20. Я хочу показать .... (подруга) новое платье.

21. Президент обещает .... (народ) новые реформы.

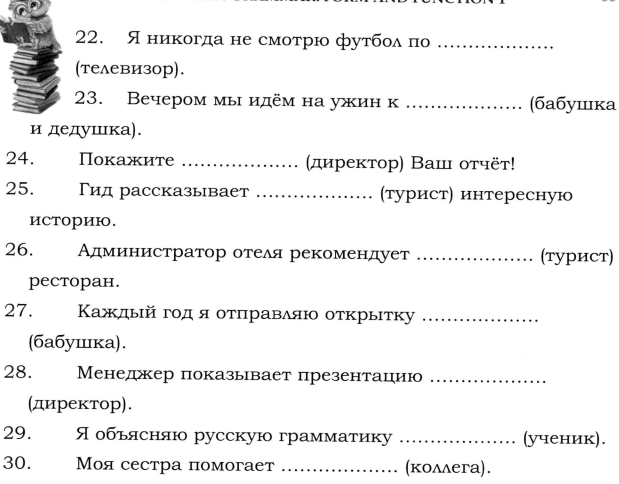

22.   Я никогда не смотрю футбол по .... (телевизор).

23.   Вечером мы идём на ужин к .... (бабушка и дедушка).

24.   Покажите .... (директор) Ваш отчёт!

25.   Гид рассказывает .... (турист) интересную историю.

26.   Администратор отеля рекомендует .... (турист) ресторан.

27.   Каждый год я отправляю открытку .... (бабушка).

28.   Менеджер показывает презентацию .... (директор).

29.   Я объясняю русскую грамматику .... (ученик).

30.   Моя сестра помогает .... (коллега).

PLURAL

	Окончания (endings)	Примеры (examples)	
		Именительный падеж (Nominative case) (singular)	Дательный падеж (Dative case) (plural)
Множествен-ное число (plural)	cons., a, o → ам	Это врач. Это студентка.	Я доверяю врачам. Преподаватель помогает студенткам.

	ь, е, я → ям	Это учитель.	Я пишу письма учителям.
		Это родитель.	Родителям 45 лет.

Exceptions

радио – радио
мать – матери
дочь – дочери
отец – отцу

отцы – отцам
друзья – друзьям
братья – братьям
сыновья – сыновьям
матери – матерям
дочери – дочерям
сёстры – сёстрам
дети – детям
люди - людям

Exercise 2

1. Кому Вы часто посылаете открытки?

2. Кому Вы пишите письма?

3. Кому Вы часто звоните?

4. Кому Вы дарите цветы?

5. Кому Вы помогаете?

6. Что Вы смотрите по телевизору?

7. Что Вы слушаете по радио?

8. Кто Вы по профессии?

9. Вы любите гулять по парку? По городу?

10. Кому нравится Москва?

11.   К кому Вы любите ходить в гости?

12.   Вы часто ходите к врачу?

13.   Кто Ваш лучший друг по национальности?

14.   Кому нужна машина?

15.   Кому гид показывает город?

16.   Кому Вы помогаете изучать иностранный язык?

17.   Кому Вы посоветовали изучать русский язык?

18.   Кому Вы дали словарь?

19.   Кому Вы показали фотографии?

20.   Кому Вы дали свой номер телефона?

21.   Вы пойдёте завтра в гости?

22.   Вы поедете в Англию в декабре?

23.   К кому Вы пойдёте в воскресенье?

24.   Вам нужно купить книги по литературе?

25.   Что сообщили по радио сегодня утром?

26.   Когда у Вас экзамен по русскому языку?

27.   Кому нужно много отдыхать?

28.   Вы вчера гуляли по городу?

29.   Кому трудно говорить по-русски?

30.   Сколько лет преподавателю?

31.   Вы доверяете врачам?

32.   Кому Вы доверяете?

33.   Кому нельзя доверять?

34.   Что нужно дарить друзьям?

35.   Что нравится котам?

Exercise 3

Что кому нравится?

Пример. Папе нравится хоккей.

мальчик/преподаватель/собака/девочка/художник/мама

Exercise 4

Это расписание Алисы. К кому она идёт на этой неделе?

Пример. В понедельник Алиса идёт к врачу.

понедельник	14.00 врач
вторник	17.00 подруга Аня
среда	10.00 бабушка
четверг	18.00 тётя Рита
пятница	11.00 фотограф
суббота	15.00 парикмахер
воскресенье	12.00 родители

DAT+ нужен/нужна/нужно/нужны + subject

Компании (indirect object/Dat.) **нужны** (verb/plur.) **клиенты** (subject/plur.).

Маме (indirect object/Dat.) **нужна** (verb/sing./fem.) **книга** (subject/fem.).

Отцу (indirect object/Dat.) **нужен** (verb/sing./masc.) **телевизор** (subject/ sing./masc.).

Студентке (indirect object/Dat.) **нужно** (verb/sing./neut.) **платье** (subject/ sing./neut.).

Exercise 5

Это Олег.

Что нужно Олегу утром?

Пример. Олегу нужен кофе.

кофе/завтрак/календарь
(ежедневник)/компьютер
(ноутбук)/яблоко/телефон

Exercise 6

Кому сколько лет?

Пример. Папе сорок лет.

папа	40
сын	7
дочь	10
мама	39
бабушка	63
дедушка	65
дядя	42

Exercise 7

Это Наталья Владимировна. Она врач. У неё много пациентов – аллергиков. Кому что нельзя есть?

Пример. Александру нельзя апельсины.

Александр	апельсины
Настя	яблоки
Виктор	рыба
Сергей	яйца
Алёна	курица
Андрей	молоко
Евгений	брокколи

Exercise 8

Кому что нравится?

Пример. Канадцам нравится зима. Русским нравится балет.

канадцы	зима, хоккей
американцы	бургеры, кино
русские	балет, литература
итальянцы	опера, искусство
японцы	рис, сакура
французы	архитектура, круассаны
немцы	пиво, сосиски

Exercise 9

Кто они по профессии?

ТВОРИТЕЛЬНЫЙ ПАДЕЖ INSTRUMENTAL CASE

SINGULAR

	Окончания (endings)	Примеры (examples)	
		Именительный падеж (Nominative case)	Творительный падеж (Instrumental case)
Мужской род (masculine)	cons.+ ом ь→ем(ём)	Это инженер. Это писатель.	Я разговариваю с инженером. Я завтракаю с писателем.
Женский род (feminine)	а→ой я→ей (ёй) ь→ью	Это мама. Это Аня. Это семья. Это дверь.	Я сижу рядом с мамой. Я еду в отпуск с Аней. Я разговариваю с семьёй. Стол стоит рядом с дверью.
Средний род (neuter)	о→ом е→ем	Это кресло. Это печенье.	Кошка лежит под креслом. Мы пьём чай с печеньем.

О→Е after «Ш, Щ, Ж, Ч, Ц»

«Цезарь» с курицей (not «Цезарь» ~~с курицей~~)

INSTRUMENTAL CASE FUNCTIONS:

- ### INSTRUMENT OF AN ACTION

Я пишу ручкой. Я ем салат вилкой. Я режу хлеб ножом.

- ### AFTER THE VERB БЫТЬ (IN PAST/PRESENT)

Он был инженером. Она была учительницей. Я буду президентом.

- ### AFTER THE VERBS РАБОТАТЬ, СТАТЬ

Я работаю дипломатом. Я работаю врачом. Он стал писателем. Он хочет стать космонавтом.

WITH PREPOSITIONS:	
С (СО)	Я люблю пироги с яблоками. Мне нравится салат «Цезарь» с курицей. Я пью кофе с молоком.
РЯДОМ	Я люблю сидеть рядом с камином и читать книгу. Рядом с домом есть большой парк.
ПОД	Под столом лежит кошка. Я сплю под одеялом.
ПЕРЕД	Перед окном растёт большое дерево.
ЗА	За домом есть красивое озеро.

- ### SEASON AND PARTS OF THE DAY

- ➤ зимой
- ➤ весной
- ➤ летом
- ➤ осенью
- ➤ утром
- ➤ днём
- ➤ вечером
- ➤ ночью

В Москве зимой холодно. В Сочи летом жарко. Я всегда принимаю душ утром. Что Вы обычно делаете вечером?

Мышка шьёт иголкой с ниткой.

Колибри рядом с цветком.

Exercise 1

1.   Англичане пьют чай с .... (молоко).

2. Русские любят чай с .... (сахар).

3. - С чем у Вас бутерброд? – С .... (колбаса) и .... (сыр).

4. Мой прадедушка был .... (писатель).

5. Кем Вы работаете? Я работаю .... (электрик).

6. Вы хотите салат с .... (мясо)?

7. Вам минеральную воду с .... (газ)?

8. Вы любите пиццу с .... (ветчина)?

9. (Лето) .... в Мексике очень жарко.

10.   Я разговариваю с .... (сосед).

11.   Они летят в отпуск .... (весна).

12.   Новый Год и Рождество .... (зима), а Пасха .... (лето).

13.   Что ты делаешь сегодня .... (вечер)?

14.   Я гуляю с собакой................... (утро) и .... (вечер).

15.   Достоевский был .... (писатель).

16.   Вашингтон был .... (президент) США.

17.   Санкт-Петербург был .... (столица) Российской Империи.

18.   Я поеду в Японию .... (осень).

19.   Я студентка Медицинского Государственного Университета, я буду .... (врач).

20.   Моя мама была .... (студентка).

21.   Я хочу быть .... (стюардесса).

22.   Я буду .... (дипломат).

23.   Мой папа работает .... (экономист).

24.   Собака лежит рядом с .... (диван).

25.   Лампа стоит за .... (кресло).

26.   Под .... (стол) лежат книги.

27.   Перед .... (дом) стоит машина.

28.   За .... (дом) есть парк.

29.   Я гуляю с .... (подруга).

30.   Я ем суп .... (ложка).

Exercise 2

Холодно ....

Маки цветут ....

Листья желтеют ....

Exercise 3

Что они делают **утром**, **днём** и **вечером**?

Пример. Утром Алина завтракает и принимает душ. Днём она …

	утро	день	вечер
Алина			
Костя			
Даша			
я			

PLURAL

	Окончания (endings)	Примеры (examples)	
		Именительный падеж (Nominative case) (singular)	Творительный падеж (Instrumental case) (plural)
Множественное число (plural)	cons., а, о → ами	Это врач.	Я разговариваю с врачами.
	ь, е, я → ями	Это учитель.	Они будут учителями.

Exceptions

мать – матерью
дочь – дочерью
отец – отцом

отцы – отцами
братья – братьями
сыновья – сыновьями
матери – матерями
дочери – дочерьми
сёстры – сёстрами
дети – детьми
люди - людьми

Exercise 4

С чем салат?

Exercise 5

С кем Вы любите...?

- ужинать
- ходить в парк/гулять
- путешествовать
- смотреть телевизор
- разговаривать
- работать
- отдыхать
- танцевать
- шутить
- готовить
- мечтать

Exercise 6

С чем Вы любите...?

- пиццу
- салат
- кофе
- чай
- бутерброд
- шоколад
- мороженое
- рыбу
- десерт

Exercise 7

С чем Вы не любите...?

- пиццу
- салат
- кофе
- чай
- бутерброд
- шоколад
- мороженое
- рыбу
- десерт

Exercise 8

Чем Вы...?

- едите суп
- едите салат
- режете сыр
- пишите письмо
- рисуете

Exercise 9

Я пью чай с _____

Я пью кофе с _____

Я ненавижу пиццу с _____

Я люблю рис с

_____

Я люблю круассаны с _____

Я хожу в ресторан с _____

Я люблю салат с _____

Я хожу в кино с _____

Я люблю фильмы с _____

Я всегда путешествую с _____

Я люблю оладьи с _____

Я никогда не ел блины с _____

Моя бабушка печёт пирожки с _____

Мне нравится паста с _____

Я ем яичницу с _____

Я живу с _____

Моя машина стоит рядом с _____

Мой любимый магазин рядом с _____

Я пишу _____

Я часто разговариваю с _____

Я смотрю телевизор с _____

Я ем гамбургер _____

Я ем спагетти _____

Я режу хлеб _____

Exercise 10

В Индии люди делают шарики из риса, они их едят .... (руки). В Мексике не используют столовые приборы, мексиканцы едят .... (руки) и с помощью кусочка лепёшки. В Чили и Бразилии даже гамбургер едят .... (нож) и .... (вилка). В Чили нельзя есть .... (руки) даже картофель фри. А жители Японии, Китая и Кореи едят .... (палочки). В Италии нельзя есть спагетти .... (ложка). В Таиланде едят .... (вилка), но её используют только чтобы положить пищу на ложку.

РОДИТЕЛЬНЫЙ ПАДЕЖ GENITIVE CASE

SINGULAR

	Окончания (endings)	Именительный падеж (Nominative case)	Родительный падеж (Genitive case)
Мужской род (masculine)	cons.+ a й →я ь→я	Это дом. Это музей. Это писатель.	У меня нет дома. В городе нет музея. В комнате нет писателя.
Женский род (feminine)	а→ы я→и ь→и	Это машина. Это тётя. Это соль.	У друга нет машины. У меня нет тёти. В магазине нет соли.
Средний род (neuter)	о→а е→я	Это зеркало. Это море.	В комнате нет зеркала. В Москве нет моря.

Ы→И after «Г, К, Х, Ж, Ч, Ш, Щ»

У подруги есть кот. (not «у ~~подруги~~»)

GENITIVE CASE FUNCTIONS:

- ## POSSESSSION

Это машина мамы. Это дом друга. Это словарь Саши.

- ## AFTER «НЕТ», «МНОГО», «СКОЛЬКО», «МАЛО», «НЕСКОЛЬКО» AND QUANTITIES

У Саши нет книги. В парке нет стадиона. У Руслана нет жены. Это бутылка воды. Это чашка молока. Это килограмм картофеля.

WITH PREPOSITIONS:	
БЕЗ	Мне нравится салат «Цезарь» без курицы. Я пью кофе без молока. Я всегда ем бутерброд без майонеза.
ИЗ	Я из России. Мой друг из Бразилии. Моя коллега из Франции.
ОКОЛО	Около стола лежит кошка. Я сижу около окна.
ДЛЯ	Это подарок для друга.
ПОСЛЕ	В Испании люди часто спят после обеда. Я люблю гулять после ужина.

У

У друга есть семья. У профессора есть много книг. У дома растёт дерево.

На небе много звёзд, но нет луны.

У озера много деревьев.

Палатка около озера.

Exercise 1

Пример.   Это библиотека университета.

библиотека/университет

книга/чашка/около

дом/озеро/у

дедушка/машина

Аня/Артём/собака

друзья / после / ужин

салат / без / майонез

мы / мыть / посуда / после / ужин

собака / смотреть / из / окно

PLURAL

	Окончания (endings)	Примеры (examples)	
		Именительный падеж (Nominative case) (singular)	Родительный падеж (Genitive case) (plural)
Множественное число (plural) мужской род (masculine)	cons.→ ов ь → ей	Это дом. Это учитель.	На этой улице много домов. В школе мало учителей.
Множественное число (plural) женский род (feminine)	а→▢	Это подруга.	У меня нет подруг.
Множественное число (plural) средний род (neutral)	о→▢ е+й	Это окно. Это море.	В этом доме много окон. Сколько на карте морей?

Exceptions

мать – матери	друзья – друзей
дочь – дочери	братья – братьев
отец – отца	дерево – деревьев
время – времени	сёстры – сестёр
деньги – денег	деревни – деревень
	дети – детей
	люди – людей
	врачи – врачей
	дочери – дочерей
	матери - матерей

NUMBERS:

1 + NOMINATIVE (один – masc. одна – fem. одно – neut.)	один стул, один год, двадцать один год, пятьдесят один стол, одна девочка, одно окно
2, 3, 4 + GENITIVE SINGULAR (два – masc., neut. две – fem.)	два стула, три года, двадцать четыре года, пятьдесят три стола, две девочки, две машины
0, 5….∞	пять столов, пять лет, двадцать шесть лет, пятьдесят восемь столов.

Add "o" or "e" between consonants in some plural. fem. nouns (usually after «ш, ж, ч, щ»):

девушка – много девушек/картошка – несколько картошек

Exercise 2

1. Я не могу есть салат без .... (соль).

2. Что Вы обычно делаете после .... (ужин)?

3. После .... (ужин) я люблю читать газеты.

4. В России нельзя приходить на день рождения без .... (подарок).

5. Паста «Карбонара» готовится из .... (спагетти, бекон, чеснок, сливки, горошек, яйцо, сыр).

6. У .... (профессор) много .... (книга).

7. Он очень бедный человек, у него нет .... (дом, машина, работа, деньги).

8. У Вас есть работа? – Нет, у меня нет .... (работа).

9. У Вас есть фотоаппарат? – Нет, у меня нет .... (фотоаппарат).

10. У студентов сегодня экзамен? – Нет, у них сегодня нет .... (экзамен).

11. У Ани есть карандаши? – Да, у неё много .... (карандаш).

12. У них будет сегодня урок по математике? – Нет, у них не будет .... (урок) по математике.

13. У директора было вчера собрание? – Нет, ... (собрание) вчера не было.

14. В прошлом году ты жил у друга, потому что у тебя не было .... (дом).

15. У меня нет .... (велосипед).

16.   Андрей – миллионер, поэтому у него есть всё. У него много .... (деньги), ... (машина), ... (вещь(ж.р.). Но у него нет .... (семья), ... (дети), ... (друзья). Он всегда работает, без .... (выходные) и без .... (отпуск).

17.   Я думаю, что буду дома вовремя, сегодня у меня немного .... (работа) в офисе.

18.   Нужно сходить в магазин, у нас мало .... (молоко) и ....(хлеб).

19.   У Алексея два .... (дом).

20.   У .... (Даша) три .... (кошка).

Exercise 3

Сколько чего?

яблоко/яйцо/стул/книга/банан/девочка/машина

Exercise 4

1. У меня в комнате есть 2 .... (стул) и 5 .... картина).

2. Вчера я работала 10 .... (час).

3. Я просыпаюсь в 6 .... (час) утра.

4. В Вашингтоне много .... (музей).

5. У него мало .... (деньги).

6. У моих соседей 3 .... (машина).

7. Он подарил ей 11 .... (роза).

8. У меня много .... (подруга).

9. На обед я хочу 1 .... (салат) и 2 .... (кусочек) хлеба.

10. Вчера мама ходила в магазин и купила 3 .... (яблоко), 5 .... (банан), 2 .... (апельсин) и 1 .... (лимон).

11. У Вас много .... (книга)? – Да, у меня дома целая библиотека.

12. Откуда Вы? – Я из .... (Италия).

13. Я живу около .... (станция) метро.

14. Я люблю готовить для своей .... (семья).

15. Мой муж из .... (Украина).

16. После .... (работа) мне нравится ходить в фитнес клуб.

17. У .... (друг) интересная работа.

18. Японцы едят много .... (овощ) и .... (фрукт).

19. Моя подруга из .... (Германия).

20.   У .... (дедушка) есть коллекция марок.

21.   Что ты видишь из .... (окно)?

22.   Ты можешь жить без .... (деньги)?

КОЛИЧЕСТВО ЛЮДЕЙ ОТ 2 ДО 7

В моей команде <u>пятеро человек</u> (Gen.).

У моей бабушки было <u>трое детей</u> (Gen.).

Из-за экономического кризиса в стране начальнику пришлось уволить <u>семеро сотрудников</u> (Gen.).

В этой группе <u>шестеро музыкантов</u> (Gen.).

2 человека	**двое** людей/человек	двое детей	двое друзей
3 человека	**трое** людей/человек	трое детей	трое друзей
4 человека	**четверо** людей/человек	четверо детей	четверо друзей
5 человек	**пятеро** людей/человек	пятеро детей	пятеро друзей
6 человек	**шестеро** людей/человек	шестеро детей	шестеро друзей
7 человек	**семеро** людей/человек	семеро детей	семеро друзей

Exercise 5

Сколько студентов в библиотеке?

Сколько друзей на фотографии?

Сколько человек в команде?

Сколько человек на фотографии?

Сколько детей на фотографии?

Сколько коллег на фотографии?

Exercise 6

1 ГОД

2, 3, 4 ГОДА

5...∞ ЛЕТ

АЛЕКСАНДРЕ 24 ГОДА. ВАСИЛИСЕ 5 ЛЕТ. АНТОНУ 26 ЛЕТ.

1 (яблоко, машина, ключ, стол, мороженое, парк, бутылка, стакан, кресло, картина)

_____

_____

_____

2 (яблоко, машина, ключ, стол, парк, бутылка, стакан, кресло, картина)

_____

_____

_____

5 (яблоко, машина, ключ, стол, парк, бутылка, стакан, кресло, картина)

_____

_____

_____

27 (друг) _____

32 (цветок) _____

77 (год) _____

56 (томат) _____

Exercise 7

1. У Вас много друзей? Сколько у Вас друзей?

2. Сколько в комнате стульев?

3. Как долго Вы изучаете русский язык?

4. Вы можете переводить без словаря?

5. Около школы есть деревья?

6. Для кого Вы обычно покупаете подарки?

7. У Вас много учебников по русскому языку?

8. Чего у Вас нет?

9. Чего нет в Вашем городе?

10. В Вашем доме есть бассейн?

11. В Вашем доме есть библиотека?

12. Вы пьёте стакан воды или стакан молока утром?

13. Что Вы обычно делаете после ужина?

14. Что Вы делаете после работы?

15. Из какой Вы страны?

Exercise 8

Это очень маленькая деревня. Здесь нет .... (больница), есть только два .... (врач). В деревне нет .... (кинотеатр) и .... (библиотека).

Здесь нет .... (супермаркет), только маленький магазин, в котором никогда ничего нет: нет .... (хлеб), нет .... (вода), нет .... (мясо), нет .... (рыба), нет .... (фрукты). Но зато в этой деревне есть море, около .... (море) всего несколько .... (дом), поэтому люди живут без .... (шум) и без .... (суета).

Exercise 9

Без чего Вы не можете жить?

- образование
- книги
- бассейн
- отпуск
- фильмы
- музыка
- деньги
- работа
- семья
- солнце
- кофе
- машина
- шоколад
- хлеб
- друзья
- путешествие

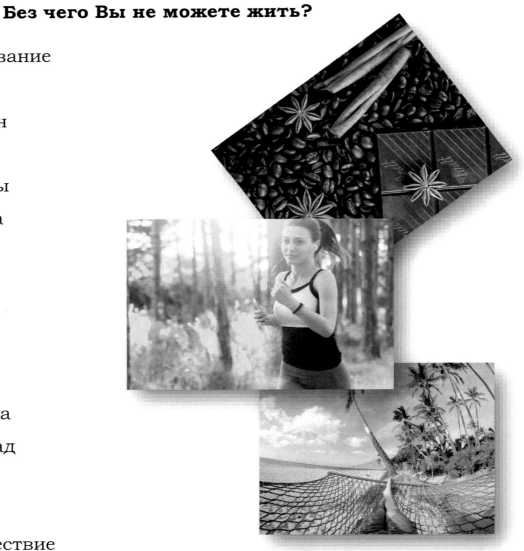

КЛЮЧИ

NOMINATIVE CASE

1.

он	чай, музей, дедушка, журнал, город, карандаш, друг, банк, врач, стол, интернет, папа, сын, кот, огурец
она	собака, профессия, мать, машина, подруга, фамилия, кошка, черепаха, бабушка, книга, дочь, утка
оно	окно, море, время, дерево

2.

он	кот, пингвин, лимон, ананас, круассан, чай, сыр, виноград, кофе
она	кошка, птица, сова, собака, рыба, клубника, ложка, кукуруза, вода
оно	яблоко, яйцо

3.

1. Врач - врачи
2. Имя – имена
3. Друг – друзья
4. Подруга – подруги
5. Музей – музеи
6. Галерея – галереи
7. Город – города
8. Мама – мамы
9. Мать – матери
10.   Стол – столы
11.   Стул –стулья

12.   Словарь – словари
13.   Игра – игры
14.   Дом – дома
15.   Лампа – лампы
16.   Ложка – ложки
17.   Птица – птицы
18.   Яблоко – яблоки
19.   Здание – здании
20.   Фотография – фотографии
21.   Лекция – лекции
22.   Карандаш – карандаши
23.   День – дни
24.   Неделя – недели
25.   Аудитория – аудитории
26.   Письмо – письма
27.   Преподаватель – преподаватели
28.   Студент – студенты
29.   Ребёнок – дети
30.   Человек – люди
31.   Газета – газеты
32.   Нож – ножи
33.   Деревня – деревни
34.   Аптека – аптеки
35.   Парк – парки
36.   Магазин - магазины
37.   Сестра - сёстры
38.   Фильм – фильмы
39.   Мальчик – мальчики
40.   Песня - песни

4.

деревья, сёстры/девочки, книги, котята, птицы, руки

PREPOSITIONAL CASE

1.

1. Где ты живёшь? – Я живу в Вашингтоне.

2. Моя сестра работает в библиотеке.

3. В августе я был в Италии.

4. Дети играют на улице.

5. Мой брат учится в университете.

6. Ты хочешь жить в России?

7. Где мой словарь? – Он лежит на столе.

8. Вчера мы ужинали во французском ресторане.

9. Ты часто бегаешь в парке?

10. Мой папа – посол. Он работает в посольстве.

11. Во Владивостоке хорошая погода в августе и сентябре.

12. Я часто отдыхаю в Испании и Греции.

13. Она секретарь, она работает в офисе.

14. Моя подруга живёт в Германии.

15. Где Лувр? – Лувр в Париже.

16. Где Кремль? – Кремль в Москве.

17. Где живут кенгуру? – Кенгуру живут в Австралии.

18. Мы вчера были в зоопарке.

19. Он всегда много рассказывает о семье.

20. Я часто езжу на работу на автобусе.

2.

Привет! Меня зовут Анна. Я люблю путешествовать.

В декабре я была в Японии.

В марте я была в Лондоне.

В апреле я была в Праге.

В июне я была в Ирландии.

В сентябре я была в Финляндии.

3.

1. Где ноутбук? – Ноутбук на столе.

2. Где очки? – Очки на книге.

3. Где книги? – Книги на полке.

4. Где машина? – Машина в гараже.

5. Где мужчина? – Мужчина в галерее.

6. Где яблоко? – Яблоко на дереве.

7. Где собака? – Собака в парке.

8. Где девочка? – Девочка на дереве.

4.

Где плавает черепаха? – Черепаха плавает в море (в океане, в воде).

Где отдыхает девушка? –
Девушка отдыхает на пляже.

Где лодка? – Лодка на воде (в море).

Где собор? – Собор в Москве (на
площади).

Где они играют? – Они играют на
стадионе.

Где студенты? – Студенты на лекции
(в университете).

5. Answers may vary.

О чём он говорит? – Он говорит о политике.

О чём они говорят? – Они говорят о природе/погоде/семье.

О чём они говорят? – Они говорят о жизни/работе.

О чём она думает? – Она думает об учёбе.

О чём она мечтает? – Она мечтает о любви.

О чём он читает? – Он читает о бизнесе.

6.

1. Говорят, что на Марсе была жизнь.
2. Вчера мы были на балете.
3. Мой папа работает на фабрике.
4. Они живут в Аргентине.
5. Мальчики играют в футбол на стадионе.
6. Я никогда не была на севере России.
7. Я работаю в библиотеке.
8. Мой сын учится в университете.
9. Ребёнок играет на полу.
10. В прошлом году мы отдыхали в Крыму на море.
11. Я так давно не был в театре!
12. В аэропорту было очень много туристов.
13. Диван стоит в углу.
14. Я учусь в университете, на филологическом факультете.
15. На улице идёт дождь.
16. Я всегда покупаю овощи на рынке.
17. Что ты обычно делаешь на даче? – Я работаю в саду.
18. Почему ты сидишь на полу?
19. Моя мама работает на почте.
20. Вчера я очень устал на работе.

8.

1. Люди живут в городах.
2. Студенты учатся в университетах.
3. Я рассказываю о братьях.
4. Бабушка любит говорить о внуках.
5. Информацию можно найти в книгах.
6. Я должен подумать о словах мамы.

7.   Я не люблю говорить о фильмах.

8.   В странах Европы все говорят на нескольких языках.

9.   Я думаю о проблемах.

10.   Они ужинают в ресторанах.

ACCUSATIVE CASE

1.

1. Бабушка читает книгу.

2. Я покупаю хлеб и курицу.

3. Мы смотрим интересный фильм.

4. Я люблю молоко.

5. Я хочу пасту и сок.

6. Я не слушаю рок, я слушаю классику.

7. Я изучаю генетику.

8. Ты хочешь кофе?

9. Что ты читаешь? – Я читаю детектив.

10.   Моя мама никогда не смотрит рекламу.

11.   В субботу я играю в футбол с друзьями.

12.   В пятницу я иду в театр.

13.   Сегодня мы идём в ресторан.

14.   Вчера мы были на выставке, а сегодня идём на оперу.

15.   Куда Вы идёте в понедельник? – Мы идём в музей.

2.

Собака любит кошку.

Попугай не любит кошку.

Они любят рыбалку.

Она купила матрёшку.

Она слушает музыку.

Он читает газету.

Они продали дом.

3.

В понедельник Ася купила юбку. Во вторник Ася купила платье. В среду Ася купила блузку. В четверг Ася купила сумку. В пятницу Ася купила сувенир. В субботу Ася купила картину. В воскресенье Ася купила календарь.

4.

В понедельник они ездили на пляж. Во вторник они ездили/ходили в библиотеку. В среду они ходили в ресторан. В четверг они ходили в кафе. В пятницу они ходили в театр. В субботу они ходили в галерею. В воскресенье они ездили в деревню.

6.

В августе Максим едет в Норвегию. В марте Максим едет в Германию. В декабре Максим едет в Италию. В сентябре Максим едет в Индонезию. В апреле Максим едет в Мексику.

7.

1. Я готовлю салат, пиццу, суп, лазанью, десерт, мясо, рыбу.

2. Я слушаю новости, радио, музыку, концерт, оперу, интервью.

3. Я играю в футбол, баскетбол, гольф, волейбол, шахматы, хоккей.

4. Я хожу в библиотеку, магазин, парк, ресторан, театр.

5. Я хожу на работу, балет, оперу, ужин, концерт.

6. Я читаю книгу, журнал, газету, статью, письмо.

7. Я пишу письмо, блог, отчёт, стихотворение.

8. Я смотрю фильм, новости, телевизор, сериал, детектив.

9. Я люблю фрукты, вино, чай, сыр, мороженое, шоколад.

10. Я ненавижу брокколи, капусту, майонез, бутерброды.

8.

Куда муж и жена идут вечером? – Они идут в ресторан.

Куда студент идёт сегодня? – Он идёт в библиотеку.

Куда они идут сегодня вечером? – Они идут на балет.

Куда мы идём завтра? – Мы идём в парк.

DATIVE CASE

1.

1. Папа дарит цветы маме.
2. Врач помогает пациенту.
3. Дедушке холодно.
4. Бабушке неинтересно играть в компьютерные игры.
5. Аня и Оля гуляют по парку.
6. Мой муж – инженер по профессии.
7. Вы часто слушаете новости по радио.
8. Вы покупаете шоколад сыну?
9. Что Вы дарите жене на день рождения?
10. Вы плохо выглядите, Вы должны идти к врачу.
11. Туристы гуляют по городу.
12. Кошке нравится играть.
13. Туристу нравится Красная площадь.
14. Дедушке нравится исторический музей.
15. Моя мама каждый день разговаривает по телефону.
16. Моя подруга американка по национальности.
17. Писателю нужна бумага.
18. Студенты обещают преподавателю хорошо учиться.
19. Я верю президенту.
20. Я хочу показать подруге новое платье.
21. Президент обещает народу новые реформы.
22. Я никогда не смотрю футбол по телевизору.
23. Вечером мы идём на ужин к бабушке и дедушке.
24. Покажите директору Ваш отчёт!
25. Гид рассказывает туристу интересную историю.
26. Администратор отеля рекомендует туристу ресторан.
27. Каждый год я отправляю открытку бабушке.
28. Менеджер показывает презентацию директору.
29. Я объясняю русскую грамматику ученику.
30. Моя сестра помогает коллеге.

3. Answers may vary.

Папе нравится хоккей. Мальчику нравится футбол. Преподавателю нравится книга. Собаке нравится кость. Девочке нравится кукла. Художнику нравятся кисти. Маме нравятся цветы.

4.

В понедельник Алиса идёт к врачу. Во вторник Алиса идёт к подруге Ане. В среду Алиса идёт к бабушке. В четверг Алиса идёт к тёте Рите. В пятницу Алиса идёт к фотографу. В субботу Алиса идёт к парикмахеру. В воскресенье Алиса идёт к родителям.

5.

Олегу нужен кофе. Олегу нужен завтрак. Олегу нужен календарь. Олегу нужен компьютер. Олегу нужно яблоко. Олегу нужен телефон.

6.

Папе сорок лет. Сыну семь лет. Дочери десять лет. Маме тридцать девять лет. Бабушке шестьдесят три года. Дедушке шестьдесят пять лет. Дяде сорок два года.

7.

Александру нельзя апельсины. Насте нельзя яблоки. Виктору нельзя рыбу. Сергею нельзя яйца. Алёне нельзя курицу. Андрею нельзя молоко. Евгению нельзя брокколи.

8.

Канадцам нравится зима.

Канадцам нравится хоккей.

Американцам нравятся бургеры.

Американцам нравится кино.

Русским нравится балет.

Русским нравится литература.

Итальянцам нравится опера.

Итальянцам нравится искусство.

Японцам нравится рис.

Японцам нравится сакура.

Французам нравится архитектура.

Французам нравятся круассаны.

Немцам нравится пиво.

Немцам нравятся сосиски.

9. Answers may vary.

Она учительница по профессии. Она продавец по профессии. Они инженеры по профессии. Он лётчик по профессии. Он режиссёр по профессии. Она журналист по профессии.

INSTRUMENTAL CASE

1.

1. Англичане пьют чай с молоком.
2. Русские любят чай с сахаром.
3. - С чем у Вас бутерброд? – С колбасой и сыром.
4. Мой прадедушка был писателем.
5. Кем Вы работаете? Я работаю электриком.
6. Вы хотите салат с мясом?
7. Вам минеральную воду с газом?
8. Вы любите пиццу с ветчиной?
9. Летом в Мексике очень жарко.
10. Я разговариваю с соседом.
11. Они летят в отпуск весной.
12. Новый Год и Рождество зимой, а Пасха летом.
13. Что ты делаешь сегодня вечером?
14. Я гуляю с собакой утром и вечером.
15. Достоевский был писателем.
16. Вашингтон был президентом США.
17. Санкт-Петербург был столицей Российской Империи.
18. Я поеду в Японию осенью.
19. Я студентка Медицинского Государственного Университета, я буду врачом.
20. Моя мама была студенткой.
21. Я хочу быть стюардессой.
22. Я буду дипломатом.
23. Мой папа работает экономистом.
24. Собака лежит рядом с диваном.
25. Лампа стоит за креслом.
26. Под столом лежат книги.
27. Перед домом стоит машина.
28. За домом есть парк.
29. Я гуляю с подругой.
30. Я ем суп ложкой.

2.

Холодно зимой.

Маки цветут летом/весной.

Листья желтеют осенью.

4.

Салат с помидорами (томатами), листьями салата, редисом, сыром.

Салат с клубникой, киви, виноградом, бананами, яблоками.

10.

В Индии люди делают шарики из риса, они их едят руками. В Мексике не используют столовые приборы, мексиканцы едят руками и с помощью кусочка лепёшки. В Чили и Бразилии даже гамбургер едят ножом и вилкой. В Чили нельзя есть руками даже картофель фри. А жители Японии, Китая и Кореи едят палочками. В Италии нельзя есть спагетти ложкой. В Таиланде едят вилкой, но её используют только чтобы положить пищу на ложку.

GENITIVE CASE

1.

Это библиотека университета. Книга около чашки. Дом у озера. Это машина дедушки. Это собака Ани и Артёма. Друзья гуляют в парке после ужина. Это салата без майонеза. Мы моем посуду после ужина. Собака смотрит из окна.

2.

1. Я не могу есть салат без соли.

2. Что Вы обычно делаете после ужина?

3. После ужина я люблю читать газеты.

4. В России нельзя приходить на день рождения без подарков.

5. Паста «Карбонара» готовится из спагетти, бекона, чеснока, сливок, горошка, яйца, сыра.

6. У профессора много книг.

7. Он очень бедный человек, у него нет дома, машины, работы, денег.

8. У Вас есть работа? – Нет, у меня нет работы.

9. У Вас есть фотоаппарат? – Нет, у меня нет фотоаппарата.

10. У студентов сегодня экзамен? – Нет, у них сегодня нет экзамена.

11. У Ани есть карандаши? – Да, у неё много карандашей.

12. У них будет сегодня урок по математике? – Нет, у них не будет урока по математике.

13. У директора было вчера собрание? – Нет, собрания вчера не было.

14. В прошлом году ты жил у друга, потому что у тебя не было дома.

15. У меня нет велосипеда.

16. Андрей – миллионер, поэтому у него есть всё. У него много денег, машин, вещей. Но у него нет семьи, детей, друзей. Он всегда работает, без выходных и без отпуска.

17. Я думаю, что буду дома вовремя, сегодня у меня немного работы в офисе.

18. Нужно сходить в магазин, у нас мало молока и хлеба.

19. У Алексея два дома.

20. У Даши три кошки.

3.

два яблока/десять яиц/десять стульев/пять книг/пять бананов/две девочки/много машин

4.

1. У меня в комнате есть 2 стула и 5 картин.

2. Вчера я работала 10 часов.

3. Я просыпаюсь в 6 часов утра.

4. В Вашингтоне много музеев.

5. У него мало денег.

6. У моих соседей 3 машины.

7. Он подарил ей 11 роз.

8. У меня много подруг.

9. На обед я хочу 1 салат и 2 кусочка хлеба.

10. Вчера мама ходила в магазин и купила 3 яблока, 5 бананов, 2 апельсина и 1 лимон.

11. У Вас много книг? – Да, у меня дома целая библиотека.

12. Откуда Вы? – Я из Италии.

13. Я живу около станции метро.

14. Я люблю готовить для своей семьи.

15. Мой муж из Украины.

16. После работы мне нравится ходить в фитнес клуб.

17. У друга интересная работа.

18. Японцы едят много овощей и фруктов.

19. Моя подруга из Германии.

20. У дедушки есть коллекция марок.

21. Что ты видишь из окна?

22. Ты можешь жить без денег?

5.

трое студентов, двое друзей, пятеро человек, четверо человек, трое детей, двое коллег

6.

одно яблоко, одна машина, один ключ, один стол, одно мороженое, один парк, одна бутылка, один стакан, одно кресло, одна картина

два яблока, две машины, два ключа, два стола, два парка, две бутылки, два стакана, два кресла, две картины

пять яблок, пять машин, пять ключей, пять столов, пять парков, пять бутылок, пять стаканов, пять кресел, пять картин

двадцать семь друзей

тридцать два цветка

семьдесят семь лет

пятьдесят шесть томатов

8.

Это очень маленькая деревня. Здесь нет больницы, есть только два врача. В деревне нет кинотеатра и библиотеки. Здесь нет супермаркета, только маленький магазин, в котором никогда ничего нет: нет хлеба, нет воды, нет мяса, нет рыбы, нет фруктов. Но зато в этой деревне есть море, около моря всего несколько домов, поэтому люди живут без шума и без суеты.

9.

- без образования
- без книг
- без бассейна
- без отпуска
- без фильмов
- без музыки
- без денег
- без работы
- без семьи
- без солнца
- без кофе
- без машины

ИСПОЛЬЗОВАННЫЕ ИСТОЧНИКИ

https://gurmantur.com/fakty-o-ede/chem-edyat-v-raznyh-stranah

https://pixabay.com/ru/

https://dksovr.ru/rossiya/chem-edyat-v-raznyh-stranah-samye-neobychnye-sposoby-priema-pishhi.html

http://nextlevel28.ru/stati/stolovyj-etiket-v-raznyh-stranah/

CONTENTS

Учебное издание
Кирпичникова Элеонора

RUSSIAN GRAMMAR: FORM AND FUNCTION 1

Учебное пособие по русскому языку для студентов, изучающих русский язык. Начальный уровень (A1-A2).

Наши сайты:

Tesoro Language Center **www.tesorolc.com**

Interesting Russian **www.interestingrussian.com**

Made in the USA
Middletown, DE
18 June 2023

32818345R00064